The Religion of Good

The Religion of Good

A Wiccan's Guide to Ethical Insight for Individuals of Any Religion or None

Ivan Richmond

*If we can't find morality in an ineffable God,
maybe we can find God in ineffable morality.*

Concrescent Scholars

The Religion of Good © 2025 Ivan Richmond

All rights reserved. Except for brief quotations in a review, the book, or parts thereof, may not be reproduced in any work without permission in writing from the publisher. The moral rights of the authors have been asserted.

The right of authors as listed in the table of contents to be identified as the authors of this work has been asserted by them in accordance with the Copyright, Designs and Patents Act, 1988.

Concrescent Scholars
an imprint of Concrescent LLC
Richmond CA 94805
concrescentllc@gmail.com

ISBN: 978-1-958359-05-1

Acknowledgments

I'd like to thank Steve Tipton and Peter Coyote for their invaluable contributions, without which this book would have been greatly impoverished; Allyn Wolfe for his unrivaled expertise in all things Wicca; Donald H. Frew and Sam Webster for all they've done to teach Neoplatonism to the Pagan community; Donald Studebaker for teaching me so much about ritual and helping me connect with the Dionysian; my spiritual teacher, mentor, initiator and dear friend Valerie Voigt for teaching me all that she has and for being there when I've most needed a friend; and my parents Amy and Lewis Richmond, not only for my life itself, but for my Zen upbringing in a unique environment, and for their constant support in my writing of this book.

Contents

1 The Ethics Crisis............................ 1
2 What is Wicca, and How is it Relevant?......21
3 The Path to the Good.......................29
4 Taking Stock in the Material World.........47
5 Myth and Mythmaking........................53
6 How to Make a Ritual.......................63
7 Direct Experience of the Good..............85
8 The Journey up the Tetractys...............97
9 The Jewel to Take Home....................107
10 The Good Life............................113
   Appendices
I: Recipes for Goodness....................123
II: Creating a Personal Place of Worship...145
III: Co-creating a Circle of Imperfect Peers.....147
IV: The Virtues of a Free Society..........151
   Glossary................................157

1

The Ethics Crisis

Several cars on my curb have broken windows. My neighborhood is evidently full of criminals. It's also full of concerned neighbors. I live in a place where teenagers race muscle cars in the middle of our residential streets. People aren't always friendly. They've had too much of unfriendliness, I suppose.

I find no solace in the news, either. It's always a new story about the same thing: clashing ideologies. It seems like everyone has their worldview, everyone comes to different rational conclusions based on ideological beliefs, and thus everyone has come to feel that it is necessary to abuse (and in rare cases threaten) their political opponents.

Our political opponents are no longer limited to party leaders and politicians, either. They are our neighbors, our coworkers, and our social media "friends." Political clashes have become cultural, personal, and moral. It seems badness is not merely perpetrated by criminals and tyrants. The same neighbors who agree that we should clean up crime are vicious to each other over politics (or something else), because they see no alternative.

I don't mean to single out crime and politics, either. Badness is everywhere. At middle age, I feel like things are worse than when I was younger. Maybe that's just a trick of time. Maybe I'm remembering through rosy-colored glasses, but it feels true. I often feel like our civilization is breaking apart at the seams.

In short, the world I inhabit is normal, and I'm just another concerned citizen trying to meditate on it all. But, sometimes, when I'm walking down the coast as the sun is setting, I feel an unaccountable sense of hope.

The West, perhaps even the world, is being haunted by the invisible menace of an ethics crisis.[1] Maybe you see it, too. Like the adults who thought the emperor was wearing clothes, this ethics crisis goes unseen by all those who are too caught up in the competing ideologies of our times. It takes a great deal of perspective to observe the phantasm that most seem blind to.

---

1 I mean ethics in a very broad way. Ethics is the study of how we ought to behave, but I don't think it necessarily comes from reason. It can also be informed by

I hear secular modernists disavowing the human quest for universal ethics, and I hear the archaically religious denying the human quest for knowledge. Creationists deny evolution. Our universities seem to teach that morals are culturally relative, but many of us struggle with how we can get along with people who have different values than we do. We are all equally afflicted by this crisis, equally ignorant of it, and equally floundering in our attempts to resolve it.

I'm trying to see beyond all this to find a better way, and I hope you are, too. We need real goodness in the world. I for one don't feel we can wait for our ministers, philosophers, and academics to resolve it. Let us, you and me, put our heads together and brainstorm a solution. I have some ideas about how we can do better, and I invite you to come along with me on a journey through my thoughts about both diagnosis and solution, and to draw your own conclusions.

I only ever wanted to be an upstanding citizen, but the more I try, the more impossible it seems. I'm not always a gentleman myself, but I keep trying. When I was young, I tried a number of different religions, including Quakerism, and New Age. I also experimented with returning to Zen Buddhism, the religion in which I was raised.

Now, I'm a Wiccan priest. As our elder, Allyn Wolfe, is fond of observing, before we get too deep into a religion's mysteries, we should really figure out what the "punchline" is. That's Allyn's snarky way of talking about the most profound part of any spiritual path: you get to meet Goddess face to face, you eat God's body (as wafers) and drink His blood (as wine), you become enlightened, you fall in love with the cosmos, or something like that. Allyn's seeming irreverence is actually his way of deflecting us away from putting leaders like him too high up on pedestals. He's prodding us into finding profundity for ourselves.

For me, one important takeaway of Wicca is that we're trained to engineer our own rituals. Why? Ultimately, to get out of our gourds and come face to face with the ineffable and mysterious.

But I'm beginning to think that goodness itself is an ineffable mystery. This may sound like a strange direction to turn, but I wonder if

---

deep religious thought or by our own intuition. I will not attempt to resolve the various distinctions we make in our society between morals and ethics. I realize that social scientists distinguish morals as coming from religious or cultural dogma and ethics as coming from reason (or something like it). Then again, in reading philosophy, it seems that philosophers and students of philosophy define morality as how we ought to behave and ethics as the philosophy of morality. In common parlance, all sorts of distinctions are made. Some people just use *morality* to refer to a puritanical sense of subjects like sex. So I won't enter into this arena and try to fight for my distinction. For the purposes of clarity, though, I intend to use *ethics* throughout this book to mean ideas about how we ought to behave and reserve *morals* to refer to religious, cultural, or ideological dogma. However, I'll also use *ethics* quite often to refer to ideas about goodness informed by religious or spiritual insight or practice, as well as those informed by reason or intuition, when I'm not talking about dogma.

ritual might actually help with the ethics crisis.

For people who are not very familiar with ritual, this may sound very strange indeed. I'll unpack this thought in the next few chapters, explaining what ritual is, what it does, and why I think it may be useful.

For now, suffice it to say that Dr. John Vervaeke, a cognitive scientist at University of Toronto, describes ritual as a means of getting a handle on ineffable mysteries.[2] Thus, a ritual is more than a series of symbolic and sacred acts. In the hands of an expert, it can be a means to dive deeply into those things that are most profoundly sacred to us.

If goodness is an ineffable mystery, and ritual helps us get a grip on the ineffable, I believe that I have a great deal to contribute to solving the ethics crisis by sharing my ritual design techniques and how I use them to get a handle on my own conception of the Good.

But I'm getting ahead of myself, so bear with me. I promise I'll unpack all that in just a bit.

First, though, I'd like to explore various approaches to morals and ethics, and to discuss why I feel that we've hit a brick wall in our attempts to figure them out in the West. I think it's best to try to clearly state a problem before trying to solve it. In this case, that means laying out everything that I think isn't working and exploring why I think it isn't.

Over the years, I've studied philosophers and sages from many cultures to try to determine exactly what my ethics are. While these luminaries all have wisdom to impart, I've found that no philosophy or religion really solves the ethics crisis. Nothing except trial and error ever taught me how to be a good person. Occasionally, though, these wisdoms I've collected return to me when I need to a make ethical decisions. Sometimes I fail to live up to them. Sometimes they fail me. Somewhere between those poles, I manage to muddle through. Well, I think that's most of us.

I suspect many of us share a vague sense that there's a quality of being good, but we can't quite see it. It seems to flit about in a misty terrain like a white stag from a fantasy story. We know it when we see it. We sense that some things are good and others are not, but we're never totally surefooted.

I can see it on people's faces. So many people appear neurotic these days, worried they'll do the "wrong" thing, but not quite sure what "wrong" is. Are you right enough with the Lord? Are you woke enough with your peers? To quote the Chinese philosopher Lao Tzu, "those who know don't say. Those who say don't know".

Some people have the hubris to tell the rest of us what's right and

---

[2] See his video series, "Awakening from the Meaning Crisis", which can be found on YouTube. I hope I've understood him correctly. His video series was way over my head, but I grok that he has an excellent theory that sheds light on the spiritual practice that I've been engaged with as a Wiccan priest.

wrong, but we suspect an insecure person behind every moralistic mask. We wonder if all they want is power. Who put them in charge? Are they deliberately manipulating us? Blinding us? Abusing us? Maybe they just don't know what's good, either.

To quote Bob Dylan, "While some on principles baptized to strict party platform ties; social clubs in drag disguise; outsiders they can freely criticize; tell nothing except who to idolize and say God bless him."

None of our leaders seem to know what it means to be good. Maybe nobody knows. We might ask, why be good at all? If you're a cynic, this book might not be for you, but if you're asking sincerely, I can give you your pick of reasons. I could point out that we can take nothing with us when we die, and so all that matters is our legacy, which had better be a good one. I could discuss how all actions are bound by cause and effect. I could entreat you to care about humanity. I could ask you to meditate on the preciousness of your own consciousness and from there to realize that all other consciousnesses are equally precious.

We're all interdependent. We rely on the roads paved by others, the tools made by others, and our relationships with others to mutually survive. We have to get along with each other. It is my hope that in these pages we can chart a way forward to that beautiful city lost in the tangle of our mutual ignorance—Goodville.

I designate the problem as the ethics crisis. I describe the quest as the Religion of Good.

The Origins of the Ethics Crisis

I've been trying to piece together why it's so difficult for us to understand goodness clearly. As a fellow fallible human, I'd like to invite you to join me on this exploratory trek to see what we might find.

To understand the roots of the ethics crisis, we must go back to before it began. The year 1780, when Immanuel Kant published *Foundation of the Metaphysic of Morals*, will do. I won't try to explain Kant. It was the most difficult reading I've ever done. But I'll tell you my takeaway on that one book, rather than pretend to understand the entirety of that genius's work.

Kant assumed that nature has will and purpose given by God. He tried to approach ethics in a similar manner as scientists approach nature or as mathematicians approach numbers. He believed that morality, like nature, was universal, that the human quest to understand universal ethics was equivalent to the human quest for knowledge. No king, emperor, or pope should force an arbitrary moral system on humanity, any more than they should force scientists or mathematicians to express false conclusions about nature or numbers.

Because Kant believed ethics was as universal as science and math, he thought reason was the most appropriate organizing principle to approach it with. It followed that moral philosophers needed freedom of thought to cooperate and synergize common efforts to discover the one truth, the one ethical system, waiting behind the veils of ignorance to be discovered by humanity.[3]

Since ancient Greece, philosophers believed that the existence of divinity was obvious, and so they had no difficulty in establishing it as the premise for many arguments. Birds, for example, appear *engineered* to fly, so they must have been designed by a Divine Engineer. For Kant and his peers, the existence of God seemed self-evident and therefore a foundational part of the universal ethics he pursued.

In those days, ethics could be found in God and His masterwork, nature. Kant reasoned that nature afforded humanity the capacity to reason so that humans could reason out God's will. Universal ethics, he concluded, must be God's intended goal for humanity: not only to "know" it, but to guide our lives by it.

Then, in the 1850s, Charles Darwin, in collaboration with others, led the discovery that evolution is based on random accident and natural selection. His tightly reasoned theory threatened the underpinnings of an intelligent nature. In a Newtonian universe, which ran like a giant machine according to discoverable rules and principles, even God was no longer necessary to explain nature. Why can birds fly? Over millions of years, some animals died before reproducing, and some passed on their genes to their offspring. Over an unimaginably long span of time, some of those animals eventually grew wings and were able to fly. No intelligent design needed.

Once God, the Divine Engineer, was shrouded in doubt, the idea of an intelligence behind nature became doubted as well. Ethics had been untethered from nature or God, and if God was to be resurrected as a social force it seems it could only be in a universe which included evolution, a blind and random force requiring no intelligence to operate. Kant's brilliant argument that humanity had been *given* reason by nature in order to pursue morality was as obsolete as an extinct species.[4]

Where did that leave ethics? It would seem that ethics could only derive its existence from humanity. But if so, given the variety of human beliefs and philosophies, it would also appear that all morality was relative. In other words, morality was subject to human intervention and beliefs, and groups and individuals can determine for themselves what is signified by "the good" and "the moral."

Was universal ethics dead? This is perhaps the first glimpse of the ethics crisis.

---

[3] Well, I believe Kant actually critiqued pure reason. My only point is to discuss how sure people once were that nature and God modeled ethics for humanity.
[4] Kant is not the singular example. I could have chosen any of the philosophers from that era.

What I'm about to say is in no way meant to disparage anybody. I have deep respect for all factions that I describe below, because they're all struggling to extricate themselves from the ethics crisis. I even have a soft spot for religious extremists, because I recognize them as struggling in their own ways with a problem that, to date, has defied solution. In the end, we're all human beings caught in the mutual thrall of change, and we're all learning to live with each other.

I don't claim "goodness" as a personal prerogative. My only claim is that I also struggle with the problem. It's only been relatively recently that I perceived this problem and began to clarify for myself how humanity might band together to find a common escape. What I'm hoping for is an instructive dialogue. Maybe, together, we can find our way out of this maze.

The problem is compounded because lately it appears impossible to venture any serious opinion without offending someone. If anyone can take "offense" and close down discussion at any time, is freedom of expression ever safe? If we cancel dialogue to appease those demanding that privilege, don't we hand authoritarians silver bullets to silence descent?

Perhaps what I am about to say may sound freighted with despair, but I'm actually full of hope. I'm just trying to map out the terrain mutually so that we might formulate our strategy. And I'm hoping we'll talk *with* each other rather than *against* each other. Tolerance of diverse opinions is one of the pillars of any free society, isn't it?

Strategies for Ignoring the Ethics Crisis

We all have ways of willfully ignoring the ethics crisis, just like the emperor's new clothes. Everyone—except that one child—saw the emperor wearing new clothes because they were told he was. In the same way, we think everything's fine. (Though, if you're reading this book, maybe you're like that child.)

The strategies we use for ignoring the ethics crisis don't actually solve that much. In fact, we all pretend this gigantic problem isn't there. To be fair, though, I think the vast majority of us, maybe even all of us, do this because we see no other solution. Because there are multiple strategies, we can each learn something from others about what we're failing to face. I'll discuss these over the next few pages, as well as my proposal for the future. I hope that we come together as a species, so that we can get through this.

The Regressive Religious MacGuffin

Regressive religion in the West ignores the ethics crisis by denouncing evolution. "It's only a theory," they say. What they either fail to realize or deliberately obscure is that scientists distinguish between theory and hypothesis. A hypothesis is a suggestion about what might be true. A theory is an explanation of what we know *is* true.

What religious regressives seem to misunderstand is that scientists create rigorous experiments to prove or disprove hypotheses. These are even more rigorously peer reviewed (tested by fellow scientists). It's only after painstaking research and consensus that a hypothesis is found to be a fact. Once it is, theories are developed to explain *why* it's a fact.

It's a scientific fact that living species change—evolve—over time. Darwin's *theory* as to *how* that happens is natural selection. So, the religious regressives have stuck their heads in the sand and ignored an inconvenient truth.

I mean no disrespect in this criticism. I believe in religious freedom. People have the right to reject scientific facts. I think I can understand, at least emotionally, why someone might be tempted to deny inconvenient truths. And I actually respect the fact that religious regressives want to get up to God's Goodness and struggle with how evolution fits in with that. I think the majority of them are sincere and doing their best. Still, I cannot treat those who ignore science as if they haven't jettisoned something important.

But before we decry them, let's realize that ignoring evolution allows them to perceive universal morality in God and nature. What we can learn from them is that they often see the ethics crisis more clearly than the rest of us. They've been chased off by an inconvenient truth, because they understand the importance of being good people. While the rest of us may disagree with their approach, we can at least appreciate the problem they're wrestling with. Although we may not know it, we're wrestling with it too.

Mainstream Religious Views

More moderate or progressive adherents of organized religion accept evolution, but seem to dodge the elephant in the room in another way. A widespread religious answer to the question *Why do you believe in God?* is *I have faith*. Although this seems to get us back on track with universal ethics, I think there's a problem.

Faith is a great virtue, but I wonder if there isn't some muddled thinking here. You have to think something's real before you can have faith in it, don't you? So how can you believe in God *out of faith?* We can only have faith in God *because* we believe in God. Faith only becomes a virtue if we believe first. It is a wonderful friend when we need to be shepherded through the "valley of the shadow." But our beliefs must stand on firm ground if they are to endure.

Putting faith before belief is more sinister than it sounds. Do you have faith in one God at Whom most religions point, or faith in a "one, right, true, and only" God, all others being false? The latter starts holy wars. In this age, we see friction, warfare, and even terrorism between Christians and Jews, Jews and Muslim, Muslims and Hindus, Protestants and Catholics, and so forth. So when faith gets elevated to our sole reason for believing in God, it can quickly become a vice instead of a virtue.

However, I can understand reasons why people might have this kind of faith. If people can bring God back into the picture through a leap of faith, it would seem we don't have to get rid of evolution in order to go back to universal morality. That's completely understandable, but with all due respect to the faithful, it seems to me that faith in one-God-ism is actually moral relativism in moral absolutist clothing.[5]

Still, these folks may be on to something. They see clearly that if we found a way to think about universal concepts of goodness without involving science, we'd be on sure ethical ground again.

The Amorality Trap

Many people reason that, if we can't find morals in God and nature, there must not be any ethics at all. They go forth into the world as selfish individuals, happy to steamroll over the rest of us if they can.

The problem is that amorality offers no other answer to humanity than never-ending civil war. Just because something *is* doesn't mean that it *ought* to be. Just because nature would seem to be amoral, that doesn't mean *we* should be, too. Even if morals cannot be found in God or nature, that does not necessarily mean that we ought not have ethics.

And then many of us find that when such people fail to steamroll over us, they invariably seem to insist that they *ought* to be able to. That's very strange, because they claim not to believe in *ought*.

This underscores the problem. In fact, I think it's where ethical thinking starts. If we really believed that we could, say, steal or kill to get what we wanted, we wouldn't get to complain about others doing that to us. Would we really want to live in such a world? The solution is to start listing out things that none of us are allowed to do. When we do that, we get ethics. So ultimately most amoral people turn out to be hypocrites.

Still, we can learn something from their doubts. Doubt is no place

---

5 In other words, if each of our morals is based on religious beliefs, which are ultimately based on nothing more than faith, and that faith is in a "one-right-true-and-only-God" of our religious tribe, rather than some mysterious being beyond the ability of any religion to truly know, then in the end all we really have can be equally well described in terms of cultural relativism—Christian morals arising from Christian culture, Muslim morals arising from Muslim culture, and so on. Siloed faiths would seem to lead to siloed moralisms and siloed ideologies, which seem to be leading us right back to the wars of religion. One of my goals is to try to find some synergy by which we can all coexist within an ethically pluralistic society.

to stay, but it's an excellent way to get rid of our preconceived notions. If we only had some basis for ethics, we could climb from this doubt toward it.

Simplistic Empathy

There are a few factions that overlap both the secular and religious milieus. The first of these is the one I have to admit I'm having the hardest time criticizing. You see, it's my own chosen myopia. I still believe in empathy, but I've come to tease out some problems with only using empathy simplistically, and discarding all the other tools in my toolbox. If used in a shortsighted way, I believe it can lead us astray.

People fake their emotions all the time. Sometimes they have emotions they ignore. They can use real emotions manipulatively to pull at our heart strings to get what they want.

Even when emotions are real and valid, they're not the whole story. Our empathy can be misguided, if not deliberately yanked around. When people emotionally abuse us with false tears, real jealousy, or actual hatred, empathy can lead us straight into their trap.

Not only that, but many of the people I hear talking about empathy these days seem to care about the feelings of some much more than others. They can be, hypocritically, incredibly unempathetic to those they are blind to. So empathy can easily miss its mark.

It's one thing if a blind person bumps into us. We can imagine how hard it must be for them. We realize it's not their fault. But there are lots of ways in which overly simplistic empathy can lead to dysfunctionality.

Take our political climate, for one example. I think we've all been yelled at or chewed out unjustly by someone whose line is, *How could you say that?* They feel offended because we have a different opinion from theirs, but they make no effort to have the tolerance or self-discipline to remember that it's impossible to dialogue without differences of opinion. Democrats offend Republicans. Republicans offend Democrats. (Or substitute your own country's parties.) Any sincere opinion risks offense to someone, no matter how polite we may be. Does our empathy lead us to never express political opinions, because we might offend someone? How could democracy work if we did that?

Imagine that you post your opinion A about a political controversy on social media. Of a hundred people who respond, eighty of them flame you. Moreover, two friends call you up and tell you that your expression deeply upset them. They feel hurt. They say you shouldn't have expressed your opinion, and you shouldn't in the future, either. What ought you to have done, and what ought you to do now?

I believe that in a free society, which depends on all of us dialoguing so that we can all make the best decision at the polls, you did the right thing. However, this is not seen if we only take the emotions of the offended into consideration. If you apologized and never posted that opinion A again, you'd hurt yourself, but eighty flamers might feel better about it, and so would your two friends. Ethical calculus based solely on empathy for the offended would seem to suggest that you should never express your opinion. I feel there's something missing, though, from the idea that the emotions of the many outweigh those of the few.

Social media sites are part of our public forum. If you had said this at a coffee shop with those two friends, you might well agree to back off *with them*, but not to stop expressing your opinion altogether. But the public forum is another matter.

For me, it's more than just freedom of expression that's missing here. I believe that it serves the common good for us to dialogue in the public forum about important issues, because we, the People, run our free society best when we're all dialoguing. Assuming you were within the bounds of politeness, you did exactly the right thing by my reckoning. Your two friends and those eighty flamers lacked the civic virtues, such as tolerance and self-discipline, necessary to take a deep sigh and allow social dialogue to progress. These virtues are central to this ethical debate. If people don't want to hear your opinions, they can unfollow or unfriend you.

That does not mean we can say anything. Nobody gets to call a black person the N-word, a gay person the three-letter F-word, a woman the B-word, or a Jew the K-word. We all know it's wrong to hurt others that way.

And we know that there's a difference between expressing a sincere opinion and deliberately offending people. Moreover, the people in this example who were offended could have responded differently by saying something like, *You have a right to your opinion, but this dialogue is making me very emotional, because I feel strongly that B is the right solution to this problem, not A.* If that had been the case, you could have expressed your sympathy with words like, *I understand. This is a difficult issue that's emotional for all of us, but I hope that those of us who are inclined to can have a constructive dialogue.*

And isn't being challenged by alien viewpoints integral to our growth as members of a free society? Isn't the alternative authoritarianism? We always like to think the other side's the authoritarian one, but I think all of us have a little inner authoritarian that we need to keep in check. To quote Tears for Fears, "everybody wants to rule the world."

Here's a very different example of how I think empathy is sometimes not the whole answer. Suppose that you're in love with Sharon, and Sharon's in love with you. You've agreed to marry. However, three of Sharon's ex's—Deepak, José, and Susan—are all very jealous. They get together and suggest that all five of you enter into a group marriage. *That way, everyone's happy*, they say. You and Sharon admit that it wouldn't be totally bad as a compromise, but you feel in your hearts that you should only marry each other. Now let's set aside the question of whether or not you think group marriages are right. What should you do?[6]

I think most of us would have the intuition that you should just marry Sharon, and not because of anything against group marriages. If we simply do the ethical calculations to minimize negative emotions all around, it seems like group marriage is the right answer, though, since it will make three people more happy and two people less happy.

So where does our intuition that it's not come from? I think it comes from a deeper understanding of the problem. This isn't business, it's love! Minimizing negative emotions isn't the only factor, because love is about more than just five people's emotions. If you feel the way I do, just marrying Sharon feels beautiful and right, because the fulfillment of your love would be for just the two of you to marry, not all five of you, and fulfilling love is beautiful.

It's not that empathy as such is wrong. It's a good virtue to have. Understanding how our actions affect others emotionally is an important part of ethical thinking. I think what's going on here, though, is that there's wisdom to be brought to bear in navigating various factors in our ethical decision making. It's not as simple as tabulating up everyone's emotions. We need to shed the light of wisdom on these problems.

Whence comes this wisdom? As I'll suggest later in the book, I believe that spirituality is one source. I see empathy as a virtue we should nurture alongside others.

Shortsighted empathy fails as a solution to the ethics crisis because it fails to give us an entire ethical package. Still, if balanced against other virtues such as tolerance, self-discipline, and love (which as I'll suggest later is something I understand to be deeper and more nuanced), I think empathy must be part of the solution.

The Ethical Ambiguity of Discipline
Then, on the other side of this landscape, there's discipline. Like empathy, discipline is a virtue, but it's not the whole solution. The Nazis were extremely disciplined. They were also highly efficient mass murderers. So were the Stalinists of the Soviet Union and numerous other authoritarian regimes. So while it's true that discipline can be a

---
6 I personally know people who are now in group marriages or were in ones in the past and are quite happy that way, but that's not the point of this example.

helpful tool for good behavior, it can equally be used for bad.

That being said, most people who call for discipline are not Nazis. They see clearly what we'll need once we figure out what our ethics are. If we could just figure those out, we'd know what we need to implement them. In a free society, though, *self-discipline* is probably what we're after rather than *authoritarian* discipline.

The Nihilistic Potential of Moral Relativism

Moral relativism encapsulates the idea that morality doesn't come from God, nature, or any other universal. According to this theory, morality comes from us. Whether morality comes from individuals or cultures, there isn't really any gold standard, there aren't any ways to measure or evaluate morality, there's no moral compass, and there are no universals. Every individual and culture simply has its own set of morals and that's all there is.

When I finished college, moral relativism seemed like a liberal utopia—we could all just allow everyone the freedom to be guided by their own lights. It often seems like there are no real alternatives anyway. After a few decades of life, though, I've come to worry that it throws the baby out with the bathwater.

I know I have to tread carefully here because moral relativism versus moral realism is still an ongoing debate. Moral relativism is a very common conclusion and there are good rational reasons to conclude that it's a valid analysis. My ideas in this book do not depend on moral realism or arguments against moral relativism.

I just want to point out some caveats with it and suggest that what we may really be after in finding both a factual and workable theory of ethics is more like ethical pluralism, circumscribed by the values of a free society, which enable multiple ethical systems to coexist without civil war and ideological strife. That is, I'm going to suggest that there may be room for multiple perspectives on moral realism within ethical pluralism, and these ideas do not necessarily conflict. As we'll see, the core ideas I want to present in this book do not require one to come down on one side or the other on this debate.

All that being said, I believe that unalienable rights are universal, not relative. They are the bedrock of a free society. Moral relativism, understood in a strict sense, seems to jettison these rights, though, because the concept of unalienable rights comes down to us in universalist terms ("we hold these *truths* to be self-evident"). Many moral relativists seem to be naively playing a game of King of the Hill.[7] Meanwhile, diverse moralists wage holy wars and preemptive strikes against each other.

I know they're not doing it on purpose. In fact, I think they mean well.

---

7 Should we degenderize that as Monarch of the Hill?

The problem is that, if unalienable rights are uncertain, some other group might impose morals on you. Unalienable rights form a framework in which we can freely and peacefully discuss a variety of approaches to ethics. Without these rights, the only solution is to fight back as clashing groups of moralists try to force their ways on us.

I also worry that these moral relativists may have misapprehended ethics as being about individuals rather than relationships. If you punched me in the nose (and not in self-defense), and you have some sort of cultural justification for it, whose culture do we use to decide whether it was right? Yours or mine? Even if your culture obliges you to punch people on the nose on, say, alternate Tuesdays, that's small consolation to me and my bloody nose. So strict moral relativism does not really provide us with the tools to navigate relationships among people with different values. For that, we would need some sort of mediating principle.

Ethics are about relationships among people, not about individuals. If I were the only person in the universe, I wouldn't call the subject of how I should behave *ethics*. I'd call it *hedonism*. That is, the only question would be *What makes me happy?* It's only when we have two or more people that ethical questions arise. So it does not make sense to say that ideas about how we should get along are relative to each of us, because these ideas must take everyone involved into account.

Now, I should admit that there's another, softer-shell understanding of moral relativism, which I would call *ethical pluralism*. It's possible that it's not so much that the *only* morals are those conceived of by cultures or individuals, but rather that there are many cultural and individual perspectives on ethics, while goodness itself is a very real thing we're all struggling to perceive. As with the blind people with the elephant, maybe all of us have ethics a little bit right and a little bit wrong. So ethical pluralism does not necessarily contradict moral realism, as long as moral realists understand that there are many perspectives out there. Ethical pluralism can coexist easily with unalienable rights, if we understand unalienable rights and other free-society values in terms of guidelines that allow for the peaceful coexistence of ethical pluralism. It's only strict moral relativism that I'm challenging.

Even so, strict moral relativists have been faithful to modern reason and they should be lauded for it. If they can't find moral absolutism, they'll still have their morals, and they get to them by reason, too. With sober aplomb, they accept the facts of science and the lack of facts about God.

Now, that is not to say that I should impose my ethics on you, or you on me, or that my culture or your culture should. To be honest, I don't think any of us really knows what's right. I'm not asking you to agree with me or share my perspective. I do think, though, that I'm not alone in feeling that there's no obvious path out of this tangled mess.

I believe that true morality must begin with sincere inquiry. Rather than fighting over cultural or individual ideas about morality, I think the whole world would be better if we admit that none of us knows, we recognize our various perspectives, and then see if we, as one humanity, can figure all this out together. I'm also not sure if reason will get us all the way there.

The Murky Vision of Ethical Intuition

You may be wondering why I'm going into so much depth. *Can't we just navigate ethics intuitively?* you ask. I can understand the temptation. In fact, my proposal transcends reason, but I worry that there's a danger in raw or simplistic intuition. While it may be that philosophers give us more questions than answers with all their logic, those same philosophers warn against relying on intuition alone.

In the Nuremburg Rally, Hitler expressed his hope that the Nazi Party would rise up as a religious order that would endure for thousands of years. Fortunately, it failed. Nazism might well be said to have been driven by intuition, however twisted and ultimately *unethical* it was. It may be difficult for us, in twenty-twenty historical hindsight, to imagine how anybody would think Hitler was good, but imagine an American flag for every swastika. We must never underestimate the seduction of nationalism.

John Calvin, the founder of Calvinism, had Michael Servetus, the founder of Unitarianism, burnt at the stake for alleged "heresy." Who gave Calvin the right to decide what is and is not heresy? They both read the same Bible, and both drew different conclusions from it. The only difference was their intuition about Christian teaching.

What happens when different people have different ethical intuitions? It seems to me that there are only three possible outcomes: war, peace, or a good talk. If both parties believe that they're right and the other party is wrong, they'll go to war. If we live and let live, we'll have peace, but we may allow things we feel are wrong to go unchecked. We may also fail to understand the other person's intuitions and they'll be baffled by ours.

I think the good talk is the only truly harmonious solution that moves us forward. If you and I can sit down over coffee, tea, or beer, and explain to each other why we think what we think, I may not convince you and you may not convince me, but we'll understand one another better. I may realize that my foundations for my convictions aren't as firm as I had originally thought, and you may realize the same about your foundations. Perhaps more importantly, we may stop demonizing each other and humanize each other instead.

One Pagan group I'm a member of, Thiasos Olympikos, focuses on the Greek Gods. Its founder lives in Cobb, California, a small town near Mount Saint Helena. One year, the town experienced massive flooding. My fellow Pagans came out in ancient Greek clothing to help sandbag. After that, none of the Christians thought ill of us (even if they still think we're weirdos who dress funny). Because they saw us working for the common good, they understood our humanity. After that, our worldviews (which inform ethical intuition) mattered much less than our good character.

How do we find common ground? One way is reason. If we can explain our reasoning to one another, at least the other person will understand how we came to our conclusions. The problem is that for many of us, including me, reason only half succeeds, and may even fail. However, we can still come together and find common ground, because we can use reason as a form of communication—an explanation for why each of us thinks what we think—rather than just as a way to get at the truth.

That being said, most of us are too busy with life to spend every moment thinking deeply about ethics. We tuck those deep thoughts away for reference and just go on intuition most of the time. That's perfectly fine, so long as we check back in every once in a while and take a deep dive into ethics. Maybe what's best is to check our ethical intuition with reason and check our reasoning about ethics with intuition.

I believe that there's a deeper and more profound form of intuition. Intuition can also refer to insights or *aha!* moments that come out of deep spiritual practice. I'm going to propose that we each need spiritual practices to get our own handles on goodness—or at least that these practices are one good way to gain insights into ethics.

One difference between this sort of intuition—the kind that comes out of spiritual practice—and the raw, simplistic form I was talking about earlier is that I believe that what's really needed for ethical insight is to get beyond our egos. One good way of doing that is through ecstatic experiences.

But I'm getting ahead of myself.

While spiritual epiphanies can indeed be profound and meaningful, we must be careful to avoid pushing our epiphanies on others. How do we know we're right? The truth is that we do not. Epiphanies are best shared and discussed in a peaceful and harmonious way, rather than being the focal points of holy wars.

So that's another way in which profound and useful forms of intuition differ from shallow or shortsighted ones. How do we avoid getting caught up in ideological cults like the Nazis? We need to have enough self-esteem to have the humility to realize that just because we have an ethical intuition doesn't automatically make us right.

That's not what ethical intuitions are good for. They're good for cutting through overthinking ethical issues using reason and for seeing beyond ourselves to the broader community of sentient beings that inhabits the world.

Ethical intuition alone will not solve the ethics crisis, because someone else's ethical intuition is very likely to be different from yours—sometimes so different that you'll condemn them, if they don't condemn you first. So I think the only way through is to continue to think deeply about these issues, continue to gain insights, and ultimately continue to strive for wisdom.

That does not mean we'll reach a rational conclusion in the end. As we'll see, I have an alternative.

The Golden Rule or the Platinum Rule?

Now at this point you may be complaining that I've left out a critical thought: "Do to others as you'd have others do to you." The Golden Rule is a core Christian teaching, but it is also taught by other religions. Does it unite us?

As wisdom, I think it's great. I've been known to work with Jesus in my own spiritual practice, even though I'm not Christian. Jesus of Nazareth was one of the great wisdom teachers of world history, regardless of whether he was also God made manifest in flesh. I wonder though whether he didn't intend the Golden Rule as a general spiritual guide rather than a logical code to be carved in stone.

I was five when I experienced for the first time the problem with the Golden Rule. It was Christmas time and I had heard that I should treat others the way I wanted them to treat me.[8] At the time, my most beloved toys were glow-in-the-dark aliens and space rangers. Based on the Golden Rule, I got some as a Christmas present to give my cousin Emily.

Young children are far more honest than adults. On Christmas Day, it was clear that Emily didn't care for her gift. Sorry, Emily! When I asked my mom where I'd gone wrong (in my own little kid way), she explained to me that picking a gift meant thinking about what the other person liked rather than what I liked. The problem with the Golden Rule is that different people want different things.

Two human resources departments at two separate corporations have told me, independently, that something they call the Platinum Rule is "superior" to the Golden Rule. The Platinum Rule says, "treat other people the way *they* want to be treated." I understand that they're just trying to help, but that rule has its own problems, as well.

---

[8] Yes, I realize it may sound weird that the Zen Buddhists who raised me celebrated Christmas. It was secular Christmas, but it was also my first impressions of Christianity, because I did indeed listen to traditional carols about baby Jesus. I think my favorite is still "The Little Drummer Boy."

If someone expects us to, say, treat them with deference because of their religion, their race, their class, or the like, we don't just automatically treat them that way. Nor do we want to help drug addicts with their habits. I realize that these objections are not what the HR folks were thinking about, but it's important to vet these ethical thoughts.

While they are good ideas, neither the Golden Rule nor the Platinum Rules stands on its own as a purely rational approach. I think I know what people mean by both rules, but I worry I'm in danger of the problematic type of ethical intuition that I already think doesn't work. In trying to get a handle on ethics, I find that rules of this sort don't solve the ethics crisis.[9]

The difference between wisdom and knowledge is that knowledge is about what's true, whereas wisdom is about what's helpful. Both aphorisms are wise in some circumstances, but untrue when applied universally. If there's a God, maybe It gave humanity the Golden Rule *so that* we can perform the mystical exercise of trying to understand how our actions affect others, rather than as some purely rational statement. (Then again, maybe we human beings invented these rules. Who knows.) I just don't think we can rely on either rule to resolve all moral questions and dilemmas.

Half-Love

Another approach that many people take is just to love. That's a beautiful path, when it's done right, but there are some things to consider. I've often witnessed people, who profess to believe in love, become extraordinarily judgmental. Here's how it happens. First, they take up love as a noble standard. Then, they encounter people who are all too human. They may not run afoul of theft, assault, or any really major wrongdoing. More like, too often, we human beings aren't very nice, because none of us are nice *all the time*. In fact, we're a quarrelsome species.

If we're mature enough, we try to work things out, but with mottled success even then. On the other hand, those who put their faith in love often try to react with love, but don't get love in return. When this happens, they often become angry, even abusive, all because "holding out love" did not result in the sort of peace and harmony they expected. The troublesome people remain troublesome, and the love folks only seem to egg them on.

Trying to love everyone is a good spiritual start but, unless you're an accomplished saint, it can backfire. The truth is that for most of us

---

[9] There's also a formulation that Wikipedia lists in several variants of the Golden Rule, which is stated something like "do not do to others what you would find hateful to be done to you." I personally like that a bit better than "do to others as you'd have others do to you".

love is an emotion that we primarily feel for people very close to us: friends, family members, lovers, and so on. We can't force ourselves to feel it for other people. Sages do, but only because they've done the work to truly understand a sort of holy intimacy with all living beings. Unfortunately, love-for-all does not flow freely and unconditionally from most of us, including me.

Love is great if fully realized. But it seems to me that there's a type of half-love that jettisons nonjudgmental and easygoing behavior, which I think are important components in being a good person, too. We are all imperfect, whether God or an unconscious universe created us. It seems to me that part of being good is accepting a certain amount of imperfection in ourselves and in each other.

Now, all this is not to be confused with the wisdom that arises from a highly mystical and deeply committed practice of *agape* (divine love for all beings). From my Buddhist upbringing, I see this in the Metta practice (loving kindness meditation) of Buddhism. The goal of such spiritual practices, though, are not to provide a raw, rational account of ethics, but rather to transform us spiritually. Also, compassion (which I'd regard as akin to what I think we're really talking about with spiritual love), understood deeply, can lead us to a more mature response to real cruelty and injustice. While I don't go in for people lashing out at those of us who are all too human, I do think that love and compassion can call us to take a stand against things that we see as truly bad in the world. It can cause us to harbor Jews from the Nazis or even fight against authoritarianism or tyranny in order to liberate our fellow human beings.

I think what's missing in the simplistic conception of love is wisdom. I don't believe that love can be our only guide, because I think we need to shed the light of wisdom on all our attempts to get at goodness. As we'll see, I believe that spiritual practice is one highly effective and efficient path toward this. I'll discuss this more later in the book.

So, love is certainly another central virtue in all this, but not the whole picture: not a complete rational account of ethics. I think the appeal of love as an ethical solution is that it seems to get us to goodness without needing God or reason. It's also an attempt to fix the problems of intuition and the short-sighted forms of empathy I described above. The problem with moral intuition is that it has no explicit guiding principle. Love seems to provide that principle. The problem remains, though, that it does not in the end solve the ethics crisis.

My Proposal
I believe that humanity needs ethics, even if none of us knows exactly what that looks like. At least, I think we should return to our nev-

er-ending quest for goodness. It's understandable that everybody's ignoring the problem. We're all in the dark! There doesn't seem to be an obvious solution.

I do not claim to be perfect, not even good. I don't claim to know what's right. I only hope to make some small contribution to this dialogue by suggesting a way out and some initial steps forward. In the next few chapters, I'll lay out my solution in more detail. During the remainder of the book, I'll guide us through the journey I have in mind.

For now, suffice it to say that I think neither religious dogma, nor reason, nor intuition, nor single virtues like love, empathy, or self-discipline form the full picture. Rather, I believe that goodness is an ineffable mystery. To make sense of it, we need wisdom, and I know of one way of shining the light of wisdom on mysteries that works well for me.

As we'll see, I'd like to share Wiccan practices with you that I think will help. What I recommend is a sort of holy communion with the Good. To do this requires a serious pilgrimage of the mind to transcend the amoral vicissitudes of nature to that single and eternal point where all is one and one is all. Only from that height can we see the Good, because goodness means what is optimal for all of us.

We will never know the Good perfectly. It will take a lifetime of many such pilgrimages to even get a good handle on it, and we may do well to create regimens of daily practice for ourselves for this purpose. None of us are or will ever be fit to impose our understanding of goodness on anyone else.

My hope, however, is that we will come to a better vision of goodness, and thus become better people through this never-ending refinement of our souls. We should be more than mere individuals. We should be citizens of the world, who are informed by the unity of all conscious beings as well as by our individual wills.[10]

If you believe in God (or some form of divinity), God wants you to know the Good. If you don't believe in God, the Good is a fit object of worship, as it were. This is not a religion in the conventional sense, and I don't mean for it to be an ideology that would clash with other ideologies. Just the opposite, in fact. However, the best parts of religion—such as myth, ritual, meditation, spirituality, ecstasy, and transcendence—are the techniques that I'm going to recommend to help us get a handle on ethics. This must *not* be in a "one-right-true-and-only" way, but rather a way that synergizes a world of pluralism.

At no point will I teach Wicca in this book. However, my knowledge of ritual engineering, which I learned from over twenty years of Wiccan training, will come into play at every step, and over the next couple of chapters I'll explain why I think ritual will help with ethics.

10 Note that the word *cosmopolitan* literally means *citizen of the world* in Greek.

All religions have something to offer, and I believe that is one of the great things my Wicca can share with all spiritual people.

This journey will be one I hope we'll take together as coequals within a free society. None of us knows better than another what it means to be good, so we must walk hand in hand. This holy quest is my solution to the ethics crisis. I call it The Religion of Good.

A Meditation on Goodness

I'm going to ask you to meditate, for just a minute, on goodness. It may help to find as much quiet as you can, but if cars honk outside your home, or neighbors yell, that's real! That's human! All I ask is that you take a minute to meditate on why there's so much badness in the world and how we can even get at what it means to be good. It may not be fun, but being good is hard work. If we have any hope of solving the ethics crisis, it starts with you.

2
What is Wicca, and How is it Relevant?

As I've mentioned, I'm a Wiccan priest. So what is Wicca, and how does it relate to the ethics crisis and to the practice I'll be offering as a solution?

At this point, Wicca is extremely diverse. Wicca was designed to be a cell structure rather than a hierarchy. Each congregation (or *coven*, to use our term) is independent from every other.

So I cannot hope to encapsulate all of Wicca here. Everything I say in this chapter will be from my own perspective. And I'm not trying to convert anyone. I just want you to know about Wicca so that you'll understand how it's informed me, where it fits in with all this, and why I think Wiccan practices can help with the ethics crisis.

Wicca is a nature religion and one of the Pagan religions.[1] We have simple ethics. We celebrate the changing of the seasons and the cycles of the moon. We have a Goddess and a God, and our God is typically depicted with horns or antlers.

We also practice magic. Our Goddess has charged us to work magic for the good of the world. To us, magic and religion go together. We refer to both priests and priestesses of our religion as *witches*. It's not horror movie witchcraft. To us, the word *witch* means a spiritual practitioner.

Our Goddess has also charged us *not* to make blood sacrifices of any kind. Most Wiccans make some kind of offering to our deities. Many of us offer a portion of the food and drink we use in our rituals, many offer incense, but I think it's safe to say we all agree that offering the lives of animals is wrong.[2]

---

1 It's become a convention in my community to capitalize *Pagan* to mean modern pagan religions (even if in some way they go back to ancient times) and to use *pagan*, lowercase, to refer to non-Abrahamic religiosity from the past. This is because ancient pagans—such as pre-Christian Greeks and Romans, for example—did not actually refer to themselves in this way, whereas we *do* call ourselves Pagans. We use the term as a broad category that religions such as Wicca fit under.

2 When I was getting my Classics BA at Reed, my professors debunked a couple of misunderstandings about ancient blood sacrifice (which should more properly be called blood offerings, if we're using the Greeks' and Romans' own vo-

Like many religions, Wicca is defined by its practices rather than beliefs. So I can't tell you what Wiccans believe, because we all believe different things. Though I mentioned both a Goddess and a God just now, Wiccans have many different beliefs about who and what they are. Some are even atheists or agnostics, which is fine. What brings us together is a common set of spiritual practices, mythological concepts, and values. This also means that, when we talk about magic, we don't necessarily mean anything supernatural. Part of what many of us mean is spiritual practices. My own definition of magic is mysterious power.

Wiccan ethics is often summarized by the Wiccan Rede: "an it harm none, do as ye will". What that means literally is that, as long as our actions harm no one, we're free to follow our will. However, as in any religion, we Wiccans love to argue about what exactly that entails. What exactly does it mean to harm? Are there situations in which we're allowed to cause harm, such as self-defense, serving in the military, or eating meat, or does the Wiccan Rede imply pure pacifism? Taken literally, it actually does not prohibit harm. It only says that we're only free to follow our will *if* our actions will *not* result in harm. But in what ways are we constrained? No one Wiccan, no matter how senior or revered, can tell us, for sure, what the answers are to these questions.

It was my search for my own answers that started me on the thought process that ended up going into this book. I knew, of course, that the Wiccan Rede is more of a spiritual aphorism than a rational statement and should really be taken as such. But I wanted to gain clarity on how to be ethical, so I began teaching myself ethics (also known as moral philosophy in the universities). Let me digress, slightly, to let you in on my exploration of ethics. After that, I'll come back to Wicca and explain how that exploration has influenced me as a Wiccan priest and what I think Wicca has to offer spiritually to the rest of the world.

More than twenty years earlier, in college, I had studied the virtue ethics of antiquity, such as that of Aristotle. This is basically the concept that ethics are collections of virtues, such as courage, honesty, and patience. These need to be in proper balance, according to Aristotle, so that courage, for example, is a balance between cowardice and foolhardiness.

Decades later, my renewed interest in ethics led me to study Im-

---

cabulary). First, human sacrifice was outlawed in 80 BCE by the Romans, who had found it repugnant long before then. Second, the Greeks and Romans often cooked and ate the meat of the animals they slaughtered. We Wiccans don't go in for that, but we also recognize that, physically speaking, there's not much difference between what they did and what we do in our slaughterhouses today, except that they took better care of their livestock because they didn't want to offend the Gods.

manuel Kant's concept of categorical imperatives in *The Foundation of the Metaphysic of Morals* and John Stuart Mill's concept of maximizing happiness for all in *Utilitarianism*. I listened to lectures and podcasts on these subjects by university professors. I read *A Short History of Ethics* by Alasdair MacIntyre, partly to get a survey of moral philosophy and partly to understand his thoughts on why we seem to have failed to agree ethically in the West.

I followed that up with MacIntyre's later book, *After Virtue*, in which he further develops his idea that ethics have taken a wrong turn in modern times. MacIntyre criticizes both Kant's and Mill's schools of ethics. Kant's categorical imperatives, he thinks, can be used to justify just about anything, and the problem with Mill's ethical number-crunching to maximize happiness is figuring out exactly what one means by happiness. Emphasize one type of happiness over another and you'll radically change which way these calculations lean.

My reflections on *After Virtue* led me to this example: Should we finance heroin addicts or get them into rehab? If we think of happiness purely in terms of feeling good, we should do the former, but if we distinguish, as Mill does, between subtle and gross forms of happiness, we may conclude that sobriety is more subtly happy than addiction and choose the latter. But that leads to a new problem: what about something like homosexuality? Is that subtle or gross happiness? One can find antigay passages in the Bible (see Leviticus 18:22 and Corinthians 6:9–10 for two among multiple examples). One could take Mill's idea about subtle happiness and apply it to homosexuality as well as to heroin use. But most of us today, including me, affirm that gayness is perfectly within the bounds of ethics. So depending on how you understand happiness, different ethical calculations will become important to you.

MacIntyre likes virtue ethics because we can clearly know whether someone is exemplifying a particular virtue. It's clear what it means to be courageous, or to be honest, to take two examples. So it's less ambiguous than trying to figure out what we mean by "happiness," and it's less open-ended than categorical imperatives.

MacIntyre discovers that virtue ethics depends on how we understand two things: our purpose in being human beings, and the process of maturation that transforms us from unvirtuous human beings to virtuous ones. Finally, he appeals to us to return to earlier philosophies (particularly those of Aristotle and Thomas Aquinas) and, from there, to modernize them to give us a deeper and (to him) more workable sense of ethics.

Although I'm not persuaded by everything he says, what struck me about my reading of MacIntyre is that I also feel that the West has failed to converge on one rational means of getting at ethics. In fact, as MacIntyre points out, different people can come to *different* ethical conclusions from equally plausible assumptions and using equally valid and persuasive reasoning. That idea informs many of my thoughts in the previous chapter.

My study of ethics also led me to become very interested in the history of Wicca. That history is very murky and not at all easy to navigate, but I'll try. Scholars are still debating it. The more I learn about it, the less I know. Like many Wiccans, I was aware that a British civil servant named Gerald Gardner had discovered Wicca, when he was initiated into a witch's coven in 1939 and discovered that their form of witchcraft was, in fact, a pagan religion.

Delving into where this may have come from, I've been able to glean this much: The Western esoteric tradition, in general, derives, ultimately, from a school of philosophy called Neoplatonism that existed in the Late Roman Imperial Period. Wicca is a part of the Western esoteric tradition, so it also derives in large part from Neoplatonism. This is not a history of people but of writing and thought. Fortunately, since I got my BA in Greco-Roman Classics from Reed in 1996, I was well equipped to get up to speed.

Very briefly, my understanding of all this is that the pagan Neoplatonists were being chased away by the Christianized Roman Empire. Once Christian Emperors closed down Plato's Academy and other academies like it, non-Christian philosophers had to find homes where they and their philosophies would be safe.

They found these in the area that we now call the Middle East, in places such as Harran in what is now Turkey. As the centuries passed, Islam arose. Thirsty for ancient wisdom, Muslim leaders learned from the Neoplatonic tradition that had survived there. They also preserved the texts of the ancient philosophers, including the ancient Neoplatonists.

Muslim magicians transformed Neoplatonic philosophy into a magical practice. After the Crusades, these magic texts came into Europe and became the grimoires. Meanwhile, many Greco-Roman texts were translated from Arabic into Latin during the Renaissance. Together, these texts became a strong part of what is now the Western esoteric tradition.

Much of the Western esoteric tradition and the occult, then, is informed by Neoplatonism, and Wicca inherits from this. But what is Neoplatonism? I've put a lot of it in this book, so read on.

Gerald Gardner reported that the creed of the witches who had initiated him was in essence the Neoplatonism of Sallustius—one of the Neoplatonists of late antiquity.[3] Gardner, who was perhaps the most prominent figure ever to have promoted Wicca in the twentieth

3 Gerald Gardner, *Witchcraft Today*

century, referred specifically to Sallustius's work "On the Gods and the World"—which, of course, I had to get hold of and read.

For further reading on the history of Wicca and how Neoplatonism ended up in the Western occult, you may find two works by Ronald Hutton interesting. Hutton is a professor of history at the University of Bristol. The first work is his book *Triumph of the Moon*, which is a general history of Wicca, but it omits the Neoplatonic portion of it (I think because Hutton was not yet convinced of it). The second is found in the book *Witches, Druids and King Arthur*, a collection of articles by various scholars of Paganism.[4] Hutton's article, "Paganism in the Missing Centuries," is an account of the Neoplatonic history of Western esoterica.

Discovering this aspect of Wiccan history led me to study Neoplatonism, and in particular one concept that I believe influenced Wicca, which is a Pythagorean diagram of reality called the Tetractys. We'll explore the Tetractys throughout much of the rest of this book. My study of Neoplatonism has helped clarify the ethical teachings that have come down to me.

As I began to use Neoplatonism to shine light on the Wiccan Rede, I realized that my quest for ethical elucidation was not unique to Wicca. I believe this is something that most people, of most any religion or of no religion at all, are searching for. I'm pleased to say that I think I can do my part to help in this quest by introducing you to Neoplatonism and the Tetractys.

I have come to realize that I have something else to offer, too. We Wiccans are experts in designing rituals. We take symbols and create symbolic rituals for all sorts of purposes and occasions. We design our own rituals so often that it becomes second nature after a while. So part of my solution to the ethics crisis is to share those techniques with you. I believe that the Good is ineffable and mysterious, and that we must approach it using the same techniques by which many religions approach the Divine. You don't even need to believe in God to do this—just in goodness.

At this point, you may well be asking two important questions. First, how can an ancient diagram of different perspectives on reality—which is what the Tetractys is—be useful to our discussion? And second, how can ritual possibly help with ethics? I'll try to answer in more detail in the next chapter, but for now let me see if I can unpack this a bit.

I worry that we have lost sight of the true subject of ethics. I think our understanding of ethics comes from a sense of unity with all sentient beings. I think that's the starting point for ethical discus-

---

4 Don't be confused by this title. The book is an anthology of essays by scholars studying Paganism, and, if I'm honest, not all the articles in it seem to have much to do with the title. I highly recommend Hutton's article.

sion. How do we generate ideas about that unity? I worry that the Cartesian duality between the cosmos and the individual mind is artificial. If I look at you, you're part of my cosmos. If you look at me, I'm part of your cosmos. It's clear to me that we are both part of the cosmos, and not just our bodies but our minds and our consciousness as well. The cosmos is not dead. Certain parts of the cosmos are conscious, and you and I are two of those parts.

So there are multiple ways we can look at reality. We usually see reality as a material world in which you and I are separate and distinct. That's one valid perspective, because we don't seem to be able to read each other's minds.[5] However, I also think there's a sense in which we are all continuous with each other, as well. Recognizing this continuity helps me see the unity that I believe ethics is ultimately discussing.

I've found the Tetractys useful in understanding different perspectives on reality. As we'll see, it describes four ways of understanding reality and how these ways interrelate. This can help us shift our mindsets from the everyday perspective of us as separate and discrete consciousnesses to the more spiritual perspective of the unity of all consciousness—and ultimately of the entire cosmos. I'll describe the Tetractys in much more detail in the next chapter and over the remainder of the book.

What about ritual? As a ritual expert with over twenty years' experience, I've come to the conclusion that a ritual is much more than just a series of symbolic acts. In the last chapter, I mentioned Dr. John Vervaeke at the University of Toronto. In his video series, "Awakening from the Meaning Crisis", Vervaeke describes ritual as a form of sacred and profound drama in which we engage in certain concepts in order to try to get a handle or grip on them. For example, Vervaeke describes Lady Justice as a symbol: She carries scales, the scales are not perfectly balanced, she's blindfolded, and so on. All these things have powerful symbolic implications, but a ritual about Lady Justice is more than just a static symbol: Our interaction with the symbol helps us understand it in a participatory fashion.

I believe that the Good is ineffable and mysterious, but I also believe we can get a handle on it through ritual. Ritual allows us to enact the climbing of the Tetractys, taking us from seeing ourselves as separate, discrete consciousnesses to knowing that we all flow as one together with the cosmos. I believe we need this perspective to get a handle on unity, and we need to understand unity to get a grip on ethics. So I've come to understand ritual as a powerful tool to

---

5 I do realize there are people who believe in psychic abilities, because my spiritual community is full of them. I respect that belief, but such people will at least acknowledge, I think, that most ordinary people can't read minds, whether because they lack the psychic aptitude, the training, or both.

help us get a handle on the Good.

That's really the core of this book. Ritual technology is one thing we Wiccans can share with everyone who is searching for ethical meaning. I can help you design and enact rituals that will help you gain the wisdom and insights into ethics that I believe are missing from our contemporary debate.

In the remaining chapters, I'll explore Neoplatonism, the Tetractys, and Wiccan ritual design more deeply. This book is a practical spiritual guide, not a philosophy book, so I'll guide you in developing and practicing your own journey to the Good. If you practice another religion, you can accomplish all of this using ritual techniques that are already available to you. None of this requires you to believe in anything Wiccan, and I won't teach Wicca directly (there are already plenty of books on the market that do that).

Rather, I'll share techniques, wisdom, and practices that I've learned from over twenty years of practicing Wicca. You can apply these to your own spiritual tradition, if you have one, and if you don't, you can just apply them to your life. My hope is that all this will empower you to find goodness through spiritual means, using techniques that I think are not that different from those used by the ancient Greeks and Romans—and, for that matter, by many religions today.

3
The Path to the Good

I stand in my meditation room, facing my altar. Three angel statuettes, which I bought at a thrift store, represent the virtues of self-discipline, love, and empathy. The air sizzles as I light a match. The odor of the saltpeter gives way to the aromas of sandalwood, rose, and lavender as I light a stick of incense in front of each statue. I ask the angels to help me exhibit these virtues. I begin to chant, "I master myself! I feel for my fellows! I live in love!" I feel these virtues flow through my soul.

In the first chapter, I expressed how I sometimes feel like every path in the ethics maze leads to a dead end.

When I feel this way, it seems like no number of clergy or philosophers can ever really get us to the absolute truth about ethics or provide us with a sure ethical system. We can never have the education, the diligence, or even the fortitude to study enough ethics to become good people.

Yet I have hope that there's such a thing as real goodness. I think I glimpse it sometimes in the patterns of human relationships. I've seen it in human beings when they are just being good to one another.

We need a better way.

As I hinted last chapter, I believe there's a way out of this maze, a way to rise above it. In this chapter, I'm going to give you an overview of my solution. What I'm about to propose is not original to me. I'm just trying to put together here what I've found from ancient wisdom and show how I'm using it. It may just be that this wisdom needs a bit of refurbishment in modern times.

Traditionally, religion served those whom reason failed. Organized religions have their problems, of course, but it seems to me that some form of spirituality, more benign than authoritarian, can help us navigate ethics. Despite their flaws, religions provide myths, parables, metaphors, rituals, practices, and in some cases even ecstatic states of consciousness, all of which I believe have the potential to help us contact goodness. Let me explain.

I'm not looking at religions in terms of whether they are true or false, but rather in terms of their spiritual practices. Those practices may be beneficial to us whether or not their claims about God, angels, and the like are literally true.

We may not be able to prove that God exists, but that's not the part I find useful. The human quest for God has created a sacred imagination, and we relate to the Divine as we imagine It—whether or not It exists.

Theists who have a deep understanding of what their religion means by *God* will often describe an ineffable mystery. Regardless of whether such a being exists, I believe that religious practices have a great deal to offer us because goodness is also an ineffable mystery. I think the spiritual techniques that are meant to get us closer to God can also get us closer to goodness.

This will take a bit of time to explain. For the rest of this chapter, I'll be unpacking that thought and laying out a plan for how to use it for our purposes.

Whether true or not, myth and ritual tap into a rich symbology, so let's start there.[1] Whether or not Jesus of Nazareth was resurrected, for example, does not change that people have been finding goodness in his story for the past two thousand years (even if you disagree with certain Christian values). Whether or not Moses ever really saw a burning bush in no way discounts millennia of midrash. Mythic symbolism and ritual have real power in helping members of particular religions make sense of their values *through* the ineffable mystery of God. I think we can use mythic symbolism and ritual to make sense of the Good in a similar way.

All that being said, I believe that some new spirituality is necessary. Not literally an entire new religion, but something simpler that all of us can use whether we're religious or secular, theist or atheist. Worshiping Goodness, with all the spiritual trappings that many relate to the Divine, is a fit spirituality and a powerful metaphor by which we can approach the Good without getting mired in reason, dogma, or the simplistic forms of intuition that I described in Chapter 1.

We must *not* repeat the mistakes of the past by relying on unreliable dogma. That will only divide us. We don't need a new ideology—we already have too many, at least in this author's opinion. Instead, the practice I'm going to suggest must provide us with the myth, ritual, and ecstasy we need to get a handle on goodness for ourselves.[2] Its object is the Good itself, rather than God. If our ongoing spiritual quest makes us better people, my work here is done. All

---

1 By myth, I merely mean stories about Divinity and the supernatural, which may or may not be factually true. I am *not* using myth to mean things that are false.
2 Ecstasy is derived from a Latin root that refers to getting outside of ourselves. As we'll see, I'm going to prescribe ecstatic practices that get us to a vision of unity, which I believe will help us get a handle on the Good.

that's really required is the dedication to be the best people we know how to be.

If you do believe in Divinity, you can honor God through getting closer to the Good. Traditional religions can still rely on their holy books as sources of wisdom, inspiration, and symbology to fuel this goodness spirituality. What I'm proposing can easily be practiced alongside or as part of an existing religion.

For those atheists out there, who are turned off by supernatural ideas, don't worry. None of this will be woo-woo. I won't be speaking of the Good as any sort of spirit or God or as a conscious or volitional being.[3] When I describe this technology as spiritual, I don't mean to imply that it's anything supernatural.

It doesn't matter whether we think this goodness spirituality is factually true. We don't need to believe in it or even have faith in it. If we simply want to be good people, we need only a spiritual technology to pull ourselves up with so that we can glimpse the Good.

This Good is essentially the same as what Plato meant by the Platonic Form of Good: the Good Itself by Itself. As I'll explain, I think it exists if we look at reality from a peculiar perspective that may be foreign to you. I think the solution to the ethics crisis is not only to reach up to the Good and attempt to emulate it, but also to do so with a broader vision of various ways we can understand reality.[4]

But you don't need to fully agree with any of this philosophy or believe in anything religious for these spiritual practices to work. I bring up both philosophy and religion, but I'm not asking anyone to believe anything. The practices I'll recommend do not depend on any of this.

You can think of both the philosophy and the religious ideas I'm presenting as tools. It would be absurd to disagree with a hammer, screwdriver, or drill. Nor do we need to believe in them in order for them to work. Carpenters know their tools work as they use them. If their tools didn't work, they wouldn't use them.

My experience is that these tools work. I also realize, however, that they're very old and that they come out of times when people misunderstood many things about nature. They didn't know how momentum works in physics, how evolution works in biology, or that matter is composed of the elements of the periodic table rather than of fire, water, earth, and air.

These misunderstandings do not prevent ancient philosophy from being useful in modern ways. Rather than dismissing my practices

---

3 Although, interestingly enough, some people may believe the Good is conscious and volitional.
4 For those philosophers out there, I don't mean that I'm literally a Platonist or that I literally believe in Platonic Forms lock, stock, and barrel. It's more that I think Plato had some good ideas, and I want to refurbish them for the twenty-first century.

on the grounds that they're based on old philosophical or religious ideas that you disagree with, I ask that you test my practices, as a scientist might. Give them a good try, and see if they work.

Think of map software. We carry that technology around with us on our cellphones, and we use it all the time nowadays to navigate the physical world. But the map isn't the same as the places we go. The map is a symbol, a model of physical reality, and not the physical reality itself.

You can think of ritual similarly as a series of symbolic acts representing something sacred. Just as map apps present models of physical reality, myth and ritual can be used to model ethics.

I've said that I think the way out of the ethics crisis maze is up. That's because I believe that we get our insights into how we ought to behave from our understanding of unity among all conscious beings. Through myth and ritual, we build a ladder of symbol, metaphor, and poetry that helps us climb up to the Good in order to get a handle on goodness. Between us and the Good might stand the symbolic angels, Buddhas, saints, heroes, or what have you of various virtues. In other words, myth and ritual can help us contemplate goodness better, just as a map app helps us model our route.

Further, we can use ecstatic practices such as meditation to seek to transcend even our symbols and symbolic acts, get out of our gourds by altering our state of consciousness, and finally get an ineffable perspective on the ineffable Good.

This journey upward is the real subject of this book. Before we set out, though, it's best to have a map to get the lay of the land. The core problem of the ethics crisis, as I see it, is that we can't seem to find ethical reality in nature. But I think we've been looking in the wrong place. Instead of looking at what *is* within the harsh and unfair realities of the natural world, we'd do better to zoom out for a larger view. Let me introduce you to the Tetractys.

The Tetractys: Four Understandings of Reality

The ancient Greek philosopher Pythagoras provided us with a diagram known as the Tetractys. That's Greek for a triangular figure made of ten points arranged in four tiers. Obviously, Pythagoras loved triangles. Here's what his triangular diagram of reality looks like:

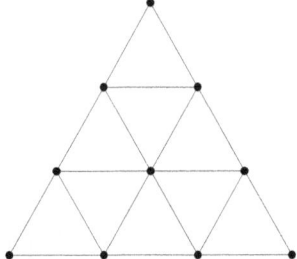

The Tetractys depicts reality at four levels. This will help us understand how we can journey from the material and seemingly amoral world of nature to the transcendent world of one-with-everything where we'll find the Good.[5] The best way to understand the Tetractys is from the bottom up.

The lowest layer is called the Tetrad, or fourth layer. This is the layer of material reality. The next one up is the Triad, or third layer, which has to do with mathematical and representational reality, which is also the reality of numbers, geometry, and patterns. We might call this symbolic reality, because it's at the level where we model the reality of the fourth level.

Next up from that is the Dyad, or second layer, which has to do with essential and abstract reality. The layer at the top—the Monad, or first layer—is the point at which we understand reality as one whole, seeing that all is one and one is all. If we can get up to that pinnacle, we'll be in a place where we can find the Good, because goodness has to do with what's good for everyone.

The key is to realize that all four realities are, in fact, one. They're four ways of describing the same thing. You can describe reality as the material world of nature (the Tetrad), or as the blueprints we use to model it (the Triad), or as the pile of abstractions we need to make sense of it (the Dyad), or as all is one and one is all (the Monad).

The ancient Greek philosophers explained it thus. A right triangle is a model of space. It's real, but it isn't material. There aren't actually any right triangles in material reality, because no lines are ever perfectly straight, no angles are ever at exactly ninety degrees, and the world is in three dimensions (at least!), not two. Thus, right triangles are not in the Tetrad.

However, right triangles *do* exist in terms of spacial coordinates. We can identify points in space and connect them. In that sense, right triangles are real. We can use our knowledge of them to do things

---

5 I should mention, now, that I do not think that transcendent is superior to manifest. I think that's a mistake, because we practice goodness in the material world. Rather, I think they're different, and it's important to know them both to make sense of ourselves and the world we inhabit.

like build temples, which do exist materially. Thus, right triangles exist in the Triad.

Moreover, the Pythagorean theorem proves that we can calculate the length of the hypotenuse (diagonal side) for *any* right triangle—regardless of size or exact shape—and *only* for right triangles. So there is a very real abstraction, or essence, which is the Right-triangle-ness that the Pythagorean theorem pertains to. Without exception, right triangles are governed by this essence. This law exists in the Dyad.

Beyond that, there are universal principles of mathematics that govern everything that math pertains to. These exist at the Monad. Thus, all four layers are valid and distinct understandings of reality.

Personally, I like how Alan Watts put it. "Reality itself is not a concept. Reality is ..."—and here Watts stopped speaking and struck a gong—"... and we won't give it a name."[6]

I'll be using the Tetractys as the map for our journey, so let me unpack all this a bit more.

The Fourth Layer: The Tetrad, or Material Reality

We all know that reality can be understood as the material world we live in: the solidity of the chair you might be sitting in and the floor that supports it, for example. This is the world of the Tetrad.

The material world is messy. Any rock I pick up is unique, even if it's made of the same granite or basalt as the rock right next to it. And a rock isn't really one thing. It once split off from a bigger rock. If I break it with a hammer, it will be reduced to smaller rocks. Is there exactly any such thing as "a rock"? Or is it more like a continuum of matter?

We aren't really single, indivisible beings either, or at least our bodies aren't. Where do we end and the air begins? Where does the air end and the next person begin? Our cells have been rebuilt several times over since we were born. So what are we?

When we try to get down to the absolute truth of the material world, we find out that it's messy, vague, and nebulous. In order to make sense of it, we rise up to the next level.

The Third Layer: The Triad, or Modeled, Symbolic Reality

When we say that the leaf of some species tree looks thus, or a flower has so many petals, we don't mean every instance of leaf or flower without exception. We mean that those attributes are coded for by genetics. Likewise a three-legged cat is still a cat, even though cats have genetic coding for four legs.

In reality, biologists could categorize species in a variety of ways, but they choose one that makes the most logical sense. This deci-

---

[6] Watts was one of the great thinkers of the mid-twentieth century. His many books helped popularize Zen Buddhism in the West.

sion is not arbitrary. We can't start calling dogs "cats". Calling dogs "dogs" is *based* on the facts of nature. This is so, even when species labels change, because these changes are in response to new discoveries.

Biologists have relabeled *canis familiaris* (dogs) as *canis lupus familiaris* (a subspecies of wolf) because the genome project shows that dog genes and wolf genes are essentially the same. Why are there all these different breeds of dogs that are so different from wolves? I'm no biologist, but I think the idea is tens of thousands of years of breeding. Note the subspecies *familiaris*.

Dogs aren't wolves, either in respect to their behavior or the way they look, but they are the same species as wolves in respect to their genes. There are multiple ways we can model nature that are all accurate to our understanding of it. We human beings have to make these models in order to make sense of things. All this is slightly less concrete than raw material reality. So, while the actual material world itself is in the Tetrad, how we *model* the material world exists in the Triad. We might say that it contains the blueprints of the material world.

The Triad is not symbolic in a subjective sense (it's not like aesthetics, in which beauty is in the eye of the beholder, or like literary criticism, in which multiple readers may each have different insights into a novel), but in the sense that the Triad is the layer at which we have our model. To be valid, that model must describe reality faithfully. In that sense, the models of the Triad are true. However, models are also symbols. Our models stand in for the messier reality of the Tetrad, which is far more difficult to describe and get our minds around.

This is not to say that all our models, all our symbols of the material world, are always valid. All too often, we understand the universe in ways that are not true. The Triad contains only *valid* models of the universe. Invalid ones are false.

The Second Layer: The Dyad, or Essential Reality

The Dyad is the level of Platonic Forms, essences, and abstractions.[7] Plato said that there are certain essential ideas, which we call Forms, that underlie all the phenomena we see in our reality. For example, though every mountain is different, there is a single essence behind them all, the Form of Mountain. Plato thought that these Forms were even more real than the physical things that imitate them. Plato would sometimes say a Form that it is a thing "itself by itself."

According to the modern philosopher Alasdair MacIntyre, one problem Plato was wrangling with was that, because different city

---

7 In its Platonic sense, *Form* is conventionally capitalized, and so are the names of specific Forms.

states had different laws, justice meant something different in every polis.[8] Faced with this, Plato searched for a universal conception of justice that all the others are instances of. After all, why even refer to, say, Athenian justice and Corinthian justice with the same word if the two are completely unrelated concepts? Plato's solution was that there's such a thing as Justice itself by itself: the Platonic Form of Justice. He thought that, like Right-triangle-ness, there's an abstract, universal Justice from which all specific instances of justice are derived.

I don't know whether there's a Platonic Form of Justice, but I think Right-triangle-ness might exist. More relevantly, for the purposes of our discussion, I think Plato was onto something, even if we might not think about it quite the same way today. Today, we might talk about all this more in terms of abstractions. Consider the mathematical laws that govern physics. These laws are not things in the world, but things in the world operate according to them, as far we know.

Whatever words we use, what I'm describing is the Dyad: the world understood in terms of Platonic Forms, essences, or abstractions.

The First Layer: The Monad, or All is One

The Monad is the layer of reality in which all is perceived as one whole. Everything is ultimately, at some level, informed by the same essence of essences and Platonic Form of Platonic Forms. This understanding is not one we can typically comprehend logically, since it transcends even logic. It is the way mystics see reality.

Remember when I said that the material world is messy? One way to get at the truth of it is to think of it as all one. When we kiss someone, is it our mouth or theirs that's involved in the kiss? Where do we end? Where does the rest of the world begin?

Or try it another way. Look out your window. Absolutely everything you see is in your head. Of course, it's also outside, but your vision of it is in your head. So, where does your mind end? Does it end at the outside of your skull or at the ends of your perception? In reality, isn't it true that the image of what you're seeing out the window is actually just a phenomenon of your mind that models the world outside your window? Where do our perceptions end and cosmos begin? Maybe the mystics aren't as crazy as they sound.

The Monad is difficult to explain, but it's basically the concept that it's ultimately all one, because everything flows into everything else. In this sense, everything is one. It's not merely part of a larger whole. To some extent, nothing can really be divided from anything else. From one perspective, everything's just the vibrating strings of String Theory. From another, everything is part of the never-ending

---

8 Alasdair MacIntyre, *A Short History of Ethics*

explosion called the Big Bang. The universe is constantly expanding.[9]

My point is that it is valid to understand everything as being part of one inseparable whole. Consider that we find meaning only in terms of how we relate to the universe. Who we are requires us to be integral to the cosmos and inseparable from it. That understanding is the Monad.

These four layers of reality are not actually separate at all. The layers above the material Tetrad are not other worlds or fairylands, and no layer is superior to any other. They are simply four different ways of describing the same reality. Here are all four layers:

Table 1 -- The Tetractys

Level	Name	Description
1	Monad	All is one and one is all, the Good
2	Dyad	Abstractions, essences, Platonic forms, big picture, the forest more than the trees, virtues
3	Triad	Numbers, geometry, models of reality, symbols, both the forest and the tree, symbols of goodness
4	Tetrad	The material world, the trees more than the forest, making the world a better place

I think that the whole problem we have in finding goodness comes from the fact that we're looking in the wrong place. As it seems to me, the Good is up at the Monad, not down in the Tetrad, though it shines down through the whole Tetractys. It comes down from the oneness at the top and manifests in the material world at the bottom, just like light coming through a prism and turning into a rainbow. Even if you don't believe that there's any fundamental goodness to the universe, you might see that the human world is full of goodness (though it's full of nastiness, too).[10]

That Good comes into each person in the form of each of our per-

---

[9] That's my layperson's understanding of physics, anyway. I'm sure I got some of that physics wrong, but I think you know what I mean and my basic point about how we can look at reality different ways still stands.

[10] As an alternative, you could also describe all this from the bottom up. Relationships among sentient beings exist in the Tetrad. From these arise various guidelines of behavior that people work out. From these arise various abstractions of ethics, such as virtues. From these arises an ultimate abstraction, which is goodness itself by itself. Take your pick. This is a spirituality book, rather than a philosophy book. The philosophy is just here to help me explain the thought process that's led me to the spiritual practices I'm describing.

sonal ethics, but we get those personal ethics from discussing with others how we all want to be treated, contemplating what's best for everyone, and thinking about how each of us, as individuals, relates to everyone else. That is, our thoughts on ethics start with a contemplation of relationships. Our concept of goodness only makes sense if we understand how it applies to the whole and then see how it manifests into each relationship.

The Roman philosopher Sallustius teaches us that the universe must be fundamentally good, because we'd rather it exist than that it not. Neoplatonists like Sallustius thought in terms of a being they called the One, which is at the top of the Tetractys in the Monad and described It as being like the sun, in that it shines over everything. They described it as the Good and the Beautiful.

They thought that bad things exist in the world because everything gets messier and messier as we refract out from the oneness of the Monad. The Light of the Good gets refracted, reflected, and shone through the smoky glass of our imperfect selves, as it were. There are blockages to the light, both in the world and in our souls. The key is to find the Good in everything and try to unblock ourselves, polish our souls, and make ourselves the best possible refractions of the Good.

A more contemporary take on this might be that, when we contemplate all humanity or all sentient life as one whole, we can easily form an understanding of goodness. When we zoom in from there to our own society, we become tribalistic. Zooming further into ourselves, we become selfish. Transforming ourselves to serve the Good is the process of connecting the zoomed-out whole with the zoomed-in self, removing the shadows of ego that blind us from realizing this.

Climbing the Tetractys

Now that I've given you a map of the terrain, we're almost ready to make our expedition to the Good, together.

The goal is not to leave the material world, though. If we did, we'd all go the way of the ascetics that Siddhartha Gautama encountered before he became the Buddha. Before achieving enlightenment, or so the legend goes, Gautama practiced with some ascetic monks who only ate one sesame seed a day, drank one drop of water a day, and slept one hour a day. Gautama almost died trying to practice this. Once he became enlightened, he realized that there's a middle way: not one of greed, lust, and avarice, nor one that denies the flesh. His middle way is one that requires us to find relief from the inherent suffering of life through sitting with reality. We can't escape life, but maybe we can transform it.

So, too, we walk the Tetractys not to leave the material world, but to be good in it. Our journey does not end at the Monad. It only pauses there long enough for us to see the Good and gain some understanding of it. After we get to the transcendent pinnacle, we need to make the return journey to our ordinary lives, which are where we need the Good. We must descend back to our everyday perspective so that we can use our understanding of the Good in daily life.

This will not be easy. The journey up can be an engaging, vibrant, and visceral adventure, and there's nothing wrong with taking in the sights, as it were, as long as we remember that this is a holy pilgrimage. But eventually we come down to earth and reemerge as the best people we know how to be in the normal, messy, material world.

And it's cyclical. The first time we take this journey may be amazing, but I propose a lifelong practice. Because our perception of the Good is never perfect, we have to keep refining it. So we take the journey many times in our lives, pausing after each cycle to take stock and just live.

At first, we might start out doing long rituals occasionally. As we get better at ritual and our practices become easier, we might work on this weekly with shorter rituals. Once we've internalize the ritual, we may compact it further into a daily spiritual practice. The more frequent the practice, the greater the benefit will be over the years of our lives. Each cycle, we get better and better, as we gain more insight into goodness.

Taking the journey will not make us superior to anyone else, however. It will be more like going to another country and then sharing pictures with your friends. We'll need to let go of any arrogance about this.

I for one have faith that, together, we'll make the world a better place by taking this journey.

Here's a summary of our journey up the Tetractys.

Table 2 - Three Path up the Tetractys

Path	Techniques
Tetrad to Triad: Material to Symbolic	Myth, scripture, symbolism
Triad to Dyad: Symbolic to Essential	Ritual based on mythic symbolism
Dyad to Monad: Essential to Oneness	Ecstatic transcendence within ritual

How we each accomplish all this is up to us. For some, we may simply be able to use the myth, ritual, and ecstatic techniques of our own religion. For others, all this may be a creative project. Remember, the path to Good begins by imagining a better world. If you don't want to use any religion's symbols, use your imagination to write your own myths or mythic characters, create your own rituals, and find your own mystical techniques. What we're mostly after are not necessarily stories, but archetypal characters—like Blind Justice with her scales and blindfold, and Lady Liberty with her torch and plaques—and other rich symbolism that we can use in rituals.

Break free from a material understanding of the world and shoot yourself up to higher understandings in order to find Goodness. Just remember to always come home by rooting yourself back in the material reality of the Tetrad.

Sallustius said that a myth is a story that never was but always is.[11] All of us who care about goodness and ethics are walking this path all the time. Unless God calls us up on the telephone (and we know it's not an imposter), we have no other evaluation of spiritual progress than our own goodness.

To quote J. R. R. Tolkien, "You need not take the journey alone. Not if there's someone you can trust."[12] We can form circles of peers, and be humble enough to listen to them. In the end, though, I doubt that anyone really has any way to prove that they know any better than we do. To think otherwise would be ideological, possibly even cultish.

We were all born as imperfect beings. We will never, ever get to the point of perfect goodness. True saints recognize their own failings. Bodhisattvas hesitate before they take the final step into Nirvana, waiting for the rest of us to be ready. So we don't try to measure our progress or compare ours to others'. We only try to be as good as we can be, for Goodness' sake.

Finally, I suggest that we take the return journey as carefully as we took the journey out. The Good is nothing unless we implement it in the material world. As the ecstatic experience wears off, we come down from the Great Oneness to the layer of essences. As each ritual winds down, these essences give way to the symbols we've used for them. As myth recedes, we leave the churches, mosques, synagogues, and temples of our souls' quests for the Good, and come blinking into the sunlight of material reality.

Our work has just begun. We have grasped the Good. Now let's implement it. This is the hardest part, because the way up is romantic and exciting, but the way down can sometimes seem humdrum. As we remember that the Good gives us purpose, we realize that the return trip is, in fact, beautiful.

Back home, we can apply everything we've done so far to the true work. We strive to be good. Informed by our journey, we keep trying to be as good as we can. That's what counts. Our good deeds and examples send ripples through the sentient world.

You may also notice something interesting. Our myth, ritual, and

---

11 Sallustius, *On the Gods and the World*
12 J. R. R. Tolkien, *The Fellowship of the Ring*

ecstatic experience are full of concepts, imagery, personifications, and stories that may not be literally true. I believe that the goodness we bring back from our journey, by contrast, *is* a reflection (however imperfect) of true Good, even if we use useful fictions to get there.

This living mythology we're working with ultimately falls away, leaving us and our good nature behind. We can still reuse all the mythology, rituals, and ecstatic techniques we used on our journey, but we can also recognize that they are, in the end, only tools.

And it may be that we have an opportunity to reevaluate our symbolism in this pause between journeys. We may find that it falls short somewhere, or leads us off track at some point. We may edit old myths or make new ones. Even if our myths come from scripture, there is always room to re-envision holy books. Perhaps the first step is to reread them.

(If you're in a scriptural religion, for the love of God, please read your scripture for yourself rather than letting anyone else, even your reverend, interpret it for you. If I may say so as an outsider, I worry that "Bible study" can be a code word for indoctrination when applied to those who have never read the Bible for themselves. Read your scripture first, before listening to somebody else's interpretation. Maybe yours is a good reverend, but there are corrupt people out there.)

The next step might be to find out what exegeses or midrashim exist for the stories we're using. The third would perhaps be to have the self-esteem to write our own exegeses, maybe even exegeses of our own myths. They don't have to be as good as those of theologians. They're just for us and our peers.

Whatever path we take, the paths to the Good are more than philosophical. They have all the myth, ritual, and mysticism of religion. This practice I'm describing doesn't belong to Christianity, Judaism, Islam, Hinduism, Buddhism, or any distinct religion. It is just a plug-in, and we can add it to any religion, or none at all. Even so, religion is a good metaphor for this practice. Whatever your creed, this journey is the Religion of Good.

Example of Practice

Here's an example of how to do this practice, from mythologizing the Good, through a ritual of goodness, to arriving at a direct experience of the Good. In Chapter 1, I criticized short-sighted versions of empathy and love as not being the whole picture. I also criticized self-discipline as not actually having any ethical content. It's useful for making sure we follow our ethics, but it doesn't imply what those ethics should be. I further suggested that all three of these things might be virtues that are part of a larger whole.

My example ritual, here, expands on that thought. I said that empathy has the potential problem of allowing people to tear-jerk us. We don't need to factor all emotions into our ethical calculations. Jealousy or hatred might be two such examples. Empathy has the potential to coddle weakness, both by not expecting enough self-discipline from others and also by not being constrained by our own self-discipline to rein ourselves in from being tear-jerked.

Self-discipline would seem to have the opposite problem. It keeps us from being swayed by other people's emotions, even the valid ones that we should factor into our ethics. Moreover, it's kind of meta, in the sense that it's a good tool for making sure that we follow our ethics, but not for knowing what our ethics should actually be. In this sense, it could be used for bad as well as for good.

Too much empathy (in the simple way I've described it) and we run the risk of being tear-jerked. Too much self-discipline without additional ethical information and we run the risk of being callous and selfish. Love is more complex than either of these, and I believe it's a good mediating virtue. Love provides us the capacity to care about valid emotions (those that should be factored into our ethics), but also to love ourselves enough to not allow ourselves to be tear-jerked. Love can lead us to fight against violence and hatred, like a mother bear for her cubs.

In Chapter 1, though, I mentioned that love is incomplete because it can lead us to hate those who don't love as we think they should. On the other hand, love can mitigate between simplistic forms of empathy and vacuous forms of self-discipline. Likewise, love is also informed *by* good forms of empathy, which are necessary to provide the loving person with information about how other people feel; and love is bolstered by good forms of self-discipline, which can rein us in from hating the haters.

I've come to think of empathy, self-discipline, and love as forming a triad of virtues which, when functioning well together, help us be more ethical. As I see them, empathy and self-discipline are across from each other in that each compliments the other, while love is in the middle, both mediating between them and being informed by them. Let's suppose I want to create a ritual to bring all three into balance. Below are the steps I used to develop this.

First, however, I'll note that this comes out of my own thoughts about how these various virtues work better in harmony than apart. If my analysis doesn't make sense to you, you could supply your own thought process about ethics and, from there, develop your own mythic symbols, ritual, and chant. I could have chosen a simpler first example, but I think the ethical thought process is important and I want you to see mine. This can serve as a model for you to develop your own practices, but feel free to try this one out, too.

Step 1: Mythologizing the Good

I start my journey by moving from the Tetrad to the Triad, the realm of symbols and myths. I imagine empathy, self-discipline, and love as three angels. I'm not very good at arts and crafts, so I go to a thrift store and—yes! They have some of those little angel statuettes that used to be popular several decades ago. I imagine that the angel Self-Discipline is always in control of itself. The angel Empathy feels for all suffering beings. Love loves always and infinitely.

Step 2: Designing a Ritual

To move from the Triad to the Dyad, where abstract virtues reside, the next step is to design a ritual. How do I symbolize my devotion to these virtues? One thing I could do is offer different types of incense to each angel. For Love, I've chosen rose incense, since roses symbolize love to me. For Self-Discipline, I've chosen sandalwood; Zen meditators often use sandalwood as a meditative incense, and meditation takes self-discipline. A quick check on the internet finds a site that claims that lavender attracts empathetic angels. Good enough for me!

Step 3: Brainstorming an Ecstatic Experience

The final stage is to use something like music, dancing, or drumming to break free from our ordinary understandings of ourselves as separate beings and get us to a point at which we can perceive the Good directly by transcending up to the Monad.

I like chanting, because I can use meaningful words that enrich the symbolism. It might seem like a good idea to have three chants, one for each virtue, and after I've chanted one for a while, I could transition to the next. But I know from my Wiccan training that one chant is best. It should be something that I can remember easily and just let myself go into for as long as I feel is right. I can read it off a piece of paper at the beginning, but it needs to be something that I can soon chant from memory.

The concepts that my chant evokes should be concrete, as opposed to abstract, and the chant should be active voice, as opposed to passive. Here's my chant:

I master myself! I feel for my fellows! I live in love!

Step 4: Finishing Touches

I know from my ritual design training as a Wiccan priest that there are some other important details I'll need to work out. I know that it's best to have a quiet place where I won't be disturbed and that's free from distractions. Fortunately, I have my own temple room, a special room in my home dedicated to spiritual work.

I know that it's best to transition myself into a ceremonial mindfulness, focusing on the work at hand. I'll begin by taking three deep breaths, visualizing all negative thoughts going down into the earth with each exhale, and holy light filling my soul with each inhale.

I know that it's best to create sacred space and sacred time, to set this ritual apart from ordinary life. I can do this easily by walking around my temple room ringing a bell. I'll do this at both the beginning and end.

Now I have everything I need. I write it all down on a piece of paper as simple notes to remind myself what to do at each step. I also write down my chant, in highly visible felt tip, along with some words I want to say as I light each stick of incense. That way the words I'm planning to speak will be easy to read by candle light.

Step 5: Performing the Ritual
Next, I'll perform the ritual. I know from experience that when I really get going, I sometimes go off script, and I know that that's okay. It's important to have a plan and to follow through, but it's equally important to allow ourselves to be inspired in the moment.

My three angels are on my altar, Love in the middle and Self-Discipline and Empathy on either side, along with three censers (incense holders) with my three incense sticks. I also have handy my bell and some matches to light the incense with.

I take three deep breaths, blowing out negativity and inhaling holy light. I pick up my bell and walk around the space, ringing it. I light my sandalwood incense in front of Self-Discipline and pray, **Self-discipline, please help me to be strong and in control for the good of all.**

I light my lavender incense in front of Empathy and pray, **Empathy, please open my heart to feel for all sentient beings. Help me understand their feelings.**

I light my rose incense in front of Love and pray, **Love, please guide me to balance self-discipline and empathy, guided by love.**

I start my chant: **I master myself! I feel for my fellows! I live in love!** After several repetitions, I feel inspired to start ringing my bell in time with the chanting. This heightens the effect. I feel the power of the words. What I'm saying fades away to sounds, but, deep down, I still know what they mean. I smell the incense. The power of the ritual surges through me. I become one with the chant.

Finally, I know when the time is right to wind it down. I let the last chant come to an end, slowing it down and holding the last note.

When I'm ready, I take a deep breath to transition my consciousness toward ending the ritual. Then, I pick up my bell and walk around the room again, ringing it. Finally, I put it back on the altar and bow to the three angels. The ritual is done.

I invite you to try out this ritual, or something similar, just to get a taste of what I'll be guiding you to do in the rest of the book. As I've said, it's up to you whether you use this ritual or one like it. If my thought process doesn't make sense to you, you're free to substitute your own. You don't need angel statues. Drawings on file cards or printouts from the web will both be fine.[13] If you have no issues with the ritual, using it as is will be instructive. If you write your own ritual to suit your own ethics, you can still use this ritual as a model.

Don't worry if the ritual you design isn't as grand as you'd like. Like any art, ritual takes practice. All I'm really hoping for is for you to just try out a ritual and just get a feel for it. Over much of the rest of this book, I'll guide you in how to create and perform rituals and practices like this. These rituals will be our mode of travel on our journey.

---

13 This probably goes without saying, but do be careful with fire. Don't, say, light paper angels on fire or light your incense at the base of curtains or anything foolish like that.

4
Taking Stock in the Material World

Broken car windows! Broken news media! Broken people! A broken world! I sigh. The culture wars, the ideological skirmishes, and the cold civil wars of the great American blood feud rage on all around us, usually limited to abuse from all sides, but occasionally erupting into social, economic, and even physical violence. Ethics are important, because our political intuitions, the health of our free society, and the fabric of our public forums all depend on them.

I take some time out to read the Dalai Lama's latest post on Twitter and feel refreshed. I remember that I have a roof over my head, food in my pantry, water, clothing, and friends who love me. The sun's shining. I'm grateful.

Still, this world is so full of suffering. So much of it is unnecessary! I feel so powerless, but I remind myself that I can help in my own small ways. My personal best is enough. I remember that my own suffering helps me to have compassion for others. I find wonder and purpose in connecting with the rest of the world. If I can connect, I can be my best self and do my best to relieve suffering, as little old me.

It's time to take the journey again, but first I must prepare.

Before we take our journey up the Tetractys, it's important to ground ourselves in the material world. For one thing, we need to be secure in the material world before we set aside time out of our busy lives to devote to our spirituality. For another, the material world is where we'll ultimately be good. This is where we'll return.

Taking stock of the material world can be a significant spiritual practice in its own right, and I think it's an important one to do right now. In my priesthood, I've seen too many people use spirituality for escapism. It can seem romantic to fly up into the pure world of transcendence, but I believe it's best to ground ourselves in the murk of material reality, first and last.

To operate ethically in the world, we need the have knowledge of the mundane. Therefore, I'm going to suggest that we get well rooted in the Tetrad before we soar above it. In this chapter, I'm going to offer you a spiritual practice of the mundane. The goal is to get a spiritual handle on the material world you inhabit before you transcend it; otherwise you won't know where you've come from and where you're returning to.

What follows is spiritual advice about our relationship to the Tetrad, rather than life advice. You already know how to live.

Taking Stock of Our Livelihood

By livelihood, I don't just mean how we make money. I mean, more broadly, how we support ourselves in every aspect. Before taking our journey, it's important to make sure we have a means of supporting ourselves. This might mean having a job, being a homemaker across from a spouse who works, or having others who take care of us. (And if you're independently wealthy, lucky you!)

If you're living with parents or friends, I can think of many legitimate reasons why you might not currently be supporting yourself financially, but struggling to get there. I know people who have been or are still in that situation. I know it's not always by choice and it can be hard. There are many difficult situations that people are in.

Having the bare necessities—shelter, clothing, food, and water—is all important for spiritual work. If you don't have them, stop reading now and line them up before going further. It will be very difficult to take this spiritual journey without them.[1]

Privacy is also extremely important. Even if you have a small room, just being able to shut yourself off there will be important. The next steps on this journey can be very difficult if you don't have that.

Finally, peace and quiet are important. You should be able to arrange some place and time in your life where and when you can regularly perform spiritual practices. This place and time should be free of distractions. If you live with others, I advise that you talk with them about your spiritual pursuit and your material needs regarding it. If there's some place in your home you can use for this work, even some of the time, it would be good to discuss using that space. If you'll be doing this work on a specific day or specific time, I strongly suggest that you work out this schedule with people you're living with. Make it clear that you don't want to be disturbed during this time. You don't want anyone walking in on you, and you want the home to be relatively quiet.

If you're a parent, you may want to talk about this with your children, or have the other parent take them off your hands during these

---

[1] Then again, if you know you can't get those things right now, and books like this one are your lifeline to living authentically, even in adversity, may you find safe harbor in these pages.

times (if there's another parent in the picture), or have friends or a babysitter take care of them for a bit, even if for just an hour a week. Make sure your children won't come into the room where you'll practice, won't knock on the door, and won't call for you. Once they're under the supervision of a responsible, trusted adult, this is your time.

I also suggest turning off your phone and muting your computer during your spiritual work. You don't want to be distracted by calls, texts, social media sounds, and the like. You might want to make arrangements with your friends and loved ones, though, for how they can contact you in an emergency.

You may also have some forms of communication that you're comfortable with. For example, you might tell your family that they can text you, but that you won't be responding to those texts until you're done. Or do like me and set your mobile phone to airplane mode, and then set it back to normal afterward.

If you're concerned that your family members or the people you're living with won't be tolerant of your spiritual practices, you don't have to tell them everything. You could just tell them what they need to know. Maybe that's just that you've decided to take an hour every week for solo spiritual work, or maybe you describe it as prayer and contemplation, or meditation, whatever will make sense to them. They don't need to know all the details, just that they need to tolerate your decision and that what you're doing is important to you.

I know that everybody has different living situations. Some are more conducive to spiritual work than others. Just do the best you can. Maybe you have to do things on your own to block out the world so that you can focus. This might mean locking the door to your room, maybe putting a sign on the door advising people not to disturb you. Even if all you have in a tiny room is your bed, that's fine. Maybe you can get a meditation cushion or a pillow to sit on.

You may find it useful to block out noise so you can concentrate. If that's difficult, perhaps you can listen to music on your mobile phone, using earphones, just to block out the noise around you. If you do this, I strongly advise music without words. Something meditative like Tibetan bells or ocean waves would be ideal, but anything without lyrics will do.

I personally think that it's nice to clean up the place we do spiritual work and keep it clean. It can be a nice opportunity to give that space a makeover. Whatever says *spiritual* to you is fine. You need not spend much money, or any at all. A clean room (or a clean part of a room) will do. Spiritual decor can be accomplished very easily with items from thrift stores or the Goodwill. And you don't really need any special decor at all. That's up to you.

Before you start your journey, I recommend taking stock of all your material needs. It's a good time to just give your bank account a once-over, getting anything in hand that you need to. Just be aware of things like outstanding doctor's appointments, home repairs, and the like. This is not so much about fixing anything. It's mindfulness of the material world. I'm encouraging you to focus on this part of reality, before we focus on other parts.

Taking Stock of Health

It's also a good time to just be a bit mindful of your food situation. This might include your grocery shopping schedule, reviewing with the rest of your household who cooks when, and being attentive to your diet. You won't need to eat super healthy, have a regular shopping routine, or become a fancy chef.

It's more a matter of simply taking stock and making any changes you feel are important (or none, if you think it's all fine). So many of us don't even think about what we eat. I'm guilty of that, too, sometimes. Some of us have a diet of ramen and junk food.

I'm not here to tell you what to eat. That's all up to you, of course. I only advise being mindful enough of it to make sure you have all the nutrition you need. If you feel that you should make changes to your diet, before your journey is a good time to do it. It's basically just a matter of taking stock. We are what we eat, so I believe we get better spiritual results when we are at least conscious of our nutritional choices. Poor nutrition can make it hard to focus on spiritual matters.

The same is true of exercise. I'll suggest that it's a good time to be mindful of the exercise you're getting and deciding whether you feel you should change it. You don't need to be an athlete, but they say a sound mind is within a sound body. Even just doing a few yoga poses or going for a walk every day might be right for you. If you're disabled, I know that's hard. I have a congenital back condition, myself, so I know that for some of us just getting any exercise at all is a miracle. All I'm suggesting is to be aware of what, if anything, you're doing for exercise, and to make any adjustments you think you should make.

I also recommend just being mindful of any health problems you may have. If you have outstanding medical complaints, it may be a good time to see a doctor, or follow up on them. And, if you're sufficiently disabled that you're just not going to be healthy, but you're already doing all you can, you have my sympathy. I understand how some days we just don't have enough spoons to even get through the day. You know your body better than anyone else and I have faith in that knowledge.

This is not a medical or health book, so I'm not giving any medical or health advice here. I just think it's good, spiritually, to make sure we're taking as good care of our health as we can be before starting out on our journey. Really, it's just about balance. You don't need to be perfectly healthy; far from it. Our bodies are our temples. What happens in our minds happens in our bodies, because that's where our brains are. I'm just suggesting we take some time to take good care of ourselves.

Taking Stock of Goodness
Perhaps the most important thing we can do is to figure out what we think it means to be good, right now. Our goal is to have a direct, if ever flawed, experience of the Good. We've been examining how difficult it is to figure out what this goodness thing is. Figuring out what we think goodness is now will help us see if we've changed our thinking at the end of our first journey.

I won't ask you to journal during this experience. I hate spirituality books that tell you to journal, and I never keep journals when I read those books. However, I will ask you to write down what you think goodness means. Maybe just save it somewhere on your computer or write it down on a file card and store it somewhere. Or, if you're a journal writer, by all means write it down in your journal.

Taking Stock of Home
What I'm really trying to do here is prepare you to come home. Eventually on this journey you'll come home, so it had better be a good place to return to. By home, I don't mean a physical place. I mean our familiar perspective on the material world. It's good to take stock of home, as I mean it, and prepare it for your return. That place is really a mundane state of mind. It's what we think of as "the real world" (though in fact, as I've said, we'll be exploring other aspects of "the real world" later in this book).

So just take some time to think about the material world. You may find that you're less in touch with it than you think. We fill our brains with fiction. Some of the fiction is obvious—novels, movies, video games, and so on. Other fiction is less obvious, like fact-twisting by the news media and politicians. Even words are just symbols, which are not really part of the material world. So I'm going to suggest that you spend a bit of time meditating or contemplating the real world. Root yourself in it. As you go about your days, take a bit of time to really see reality for what it is.

One final note: this chapter should not be an obstacle in moving forward in the book. Please don't feel obliged to change so many things in your life that you never move on to the next chapter. There's a balance here, and only you know when you're ready. And maybe just having considered all these things is all you need. Your call!

A Meditation on the Material World

I invite you to mediate on the world. I like to have a bell with me to ring at the beginning and end. A Buddhist bowl bell is perfect. You may know it as a Tibetan singing bowl. But any bell is fine. So is an app. I just think it's nice to have something we make noise with to mark the beginning and end of a meditation. Clapping your hands will do.

Take three deep breaths. With each in-breath, draw in power from the cosmos. With each out-breath, breath all doubts and unnecessary thoughts and feelings down into the earth. You can pick them up afterward, if you still need them. For now, put them in the earth so you can focus on the meditation at hand.

Focus on this world, with all its imperfections. If the neighbors are blaring their music, or if there are other distractions, just take that all in. That's the real world. Focus on yourself.

How do you feel? In your body? In your mind? In your heart? Do you feel that you're a part of this world or a stranger in it? Remember that you're a part of it. You belong here. The world will just have to accept you for who you are, because you can't be anyone else.[2] You can't control the rest of the world, but you can start by making sure one part of the world accepts you, and that part is you.

Take a deep breath and let it out. Focus on the good of this world: just the simple, everyday acts of goodness, like people helping each other or speaking kindly. Think about the good things you've done recently. Think about the good things others have done for you. Be good to yourself. Include yourself in goodness. You deserve it! Goodness means more than only being good to others. It means being good to you, too, because you're a part of this.

Accept that this *is* the world. While you can't control it, you *can* influence it more than you know. Feel your power to act on this world. Focus on your ethics about how to use that power. Breath power into yourself.

Now just sit for a few more minutes and be. Stop doing, just for right now. Allow your mind to gradually stop thinking. Keep breathing and experience the world that you're in.

When you're ready, take another deep breath and end your meditation. Ring your bell (or whatever you have for that purpose). You are now ready to begin your journey up the Tetractys.

---

[2] This is not meant in any way to suggest that you don't have a responsibility to be ethical, however.

5

Myth and Mythmaking

As I go about my life, I look for mythic symbols I can use in rituals. I'm particularly interested in symbols of virtues and goodness. Thrift shops and the Goodwill are good. Sometimes, I'll just buy online. When possible, I like supporting artists and crafts people, so I'll sometimes look on Etsy or the like, or maybe go to arts and craft fairs or open art studios. I get a statuette of Blind Justice here. A little Lady Liberty there. Cupid, a Valentine, or a red candle might represent love. A white candle might represent pure goodness.

New Age stores, metaphysical bookstores, and occult shops are also useful. I like tarot cards and oracle decks because they often have useful symbols. The Justice card can work in place of a Justice figure. I also read holy books, ancient wisdom writings, and listen to the myths and folklore of different cultures for inspiration. I've collected some great Gospel quotes, passages from the Chinese philosophers, and snippets of Buddhist texts.

A Cherokee friend of mine once explained to me that their saying, "it's a good day to die," has been misunderstood by Westerners. According to her, it is not meant to evoke fierce warriors going into battle, but rather a vision of such beauty that your life is complete. A Cherokee might walk into Yosemite Valley for the first time and gasp at its beauty, "today is a good day to die." I love learning things like that.

Incenses, herbs, and oils are wonderful symbols because aromas are powerfully evocative. Rose might mean love. Lavender could mean calm. Cinnamon might mean warmth. As I collect symbols, myths, and snippets of scripture, I allow my intuition to browse and collect symbols, bits of myth, and ideas that might be useful to me in creating my own mythology of Good. In this way, I'm always creating my own mythology of goodness.

Welcome to the Triad! Your journey has begun.
What does it mean to be in a world of symbols? In a sense, we're in it all the time. Words are symbols. So are signs. Red octagons mean *stop*. Yellow triangles mean *yield* when they're upside down. If

they're right-side-up with an exclamation point in them, they mean *warning*. The icons on your computer are modern hieroglyphs. We all know that a pawn means *user*. Three horizontal lines mean *options*. A gear means *settings*. A disk means *save*.

In a way, we're more familiar with the Triad than we are with the Tetrad. Those animals that don't have language probably understand the Tetrad better than we do: It's the immediacy of smells, tastes, predators, and prey. But to us, symbols are how we interact with the things and people around us. We understand the Tetrad through the symbols of the Triad.

In this chapter, I will ask you to choose symbols of goodness. The elements of myth and scripture create for us a collage of virtues to follow, vices to avoid, characters to revere, and demons to steer clear of (or perhaps to save). I'd like to turn your attention now to how we can take ideas, situations, and characters from scripture, myth, legend, and folklore—or even our own imagination—and use them as symbols of goodness.

Many of you may be used to religions that emphasize belief. Some people believe that their holy scripture is true, at some level, whether it's literal or to be interpreted. This book isn't opposed to that at all.

Others believe only in science, math, realism, and reason. They abandon scripture, myth, legend, and folklore, because they've concluded that none of it is true. That's fine, too.

Using symbols in this way doesn't mean denying your religious convictions. Nor do you have to believe to use symbols. You can use a religious figure as a symbol whether or not you believe what the scriptures say about him or her is literally true. The same is true for angels, heroes, and so on. We could even use a young George Washington confessing to his father that he had chopped down a cherry tree as a symbol for honesty, even though we all know that the historical George Washington never really did that.

I particularly like characters from stories. Heroes, saints, angels, and bodhisattvas all make good candidates. So do archetypal characters such as Lady Liberty and Lady Justice.

Angels can work really well for a lot of people, because all the Abrahamic religions (Christianity, Judaism, and Islam) have angels in their repertoire. Other religions that are fairly inclusive, such as Hinduism, have nothing against them. Even non-Abrahamic New Agers often work with angels.

In my religion, we work with deities, spirits of nature, and our ancestors. What I look for are characters that exemplify various virtues or various tenets that we hold to be good. I don't look for anyone who presents good in its entirety. That's hard to wrap our heads around, and it's too big for any character.[1]

---

[1] I think there are better ways to get at this. Later on in the book, one of my rituals

The way to start your collection of characters is just to start thinking about different aspects of goodness. What virtues do you admire? I find it's a good idea to make a list. Then I look for characters from mythology or scripture who fit those virtues. I've already mentioned Lady Justice and Lady Liberty. We could take the angel Michael, with his flaming sword, as a symbol of self-discipline. I might take Kwan Yin, the Chinese Bodhisattva of Compassion, as a symbol of compassion.

Once you've listed mythological or scriptural figures you want to represent, go out and look for actual images of them. Statues are great, because you can put them on an altar. When I can't find statues, I've sometimes printed images off the internet and put them in a picture frame. That works almost as well. You can buy statues online. I also think thrift stores and the Goodwill are great places to look around in. They'll often have images of angels, saints, or the like.

There are several types of characters I would *not* use. First, I'm against using national symbols like Uncle Sam or Britannia. We know from history that nations are never purely good or evil. They have their own needs and desires. They rub up against other nations. They fight wars. I have nothing against anyone loving their country, but I think it's hubris to believe that any nation is so pure that its national symbols can be used as symbols of goodness rather than symbols of nationhood. I love the freedom we have in my country, the United States, but I think it would be a mistake to use Uncle Sam or the American flag as a symbol of goodness. Lady Liberty is a better symbol for freedom because all people, everywhere, can have her.

I also think we should be very, very careful about using characters from pop culture. When I was a kid, Star Wars was sacred to many. It was the epic of our era. Its creator, George Lucas, made his own film company *specifically so that* he would not have to compromise his creative vision.[2] The result was the original trilogy: a simple epic about a warrior who learns that he cannot make a physical victory against the tyranny of his world, because the tyrant and his followers are stronger than the rebels, but that he can make a spiritual victory by throwing away his sword and refusing to fight. This causes his wayward father, who has become a tyrant after being seduced by evil, to feel compassion for him and kill the tyrant, himself. As a child, I found Luke Skywalker to be extraordinarily inspiring spiritual warrior.

Since then, Lucasfilm sold out to Disney, exactly the sort of huge movie corporation that Lucas, to my understanding, originally want-

---

has humanity gathered at the crossroads of Mother Earth. That works, because it's not a direct symbol of goodness, but rather a compound symbol of us coming together.
2 At least, that's my understanding.

ed to keep out of his creative vision. When this happened, Star Wars ceased to be an epic and became a franchise for executives with dollar signs in their eyes. Say it ain't so, George!

I have nothing against entertainment. But if we link our sense of good to stories owned by for-profit corporations, we allow them to control our symbols of goodness. To do so would be to make corporate executives priests and corporations churches. So please don't put Luke Skywalker or Harry Potter on your altar.

Novels are a bit better, but still a risk. I love J. R. R. Tolkien, because he wrote his fantasy purely from his heart, with no idea that it would ever be as popular as it is now. Frodo Baggins is a great hero for modern times: He's no more powerful than any of us, he just does the right thing. He does so not because of some lofty calling, but because he wants to enjoy a quiet life in the Shire and knows that he won't if Sauron conquers Middle Earth. Beautiful!

However, the corporations now own the rights to turn Tolkien's beautiful stories into movies and TV shows. In his retelling of the story, Peter Jackson changed the Ents' wise aphorism, "don't be so hasty," into folly. Before you put Treebeard on your altar to remind you not to be so hasty (a good virtue!), I urge you to think about how much power the corporations have to twist that.

Instead, I am inspired by this quote from *The Lord of the Rings*: «All that is gold does not glitter. Not all those who wander are lost. The old that is strong does not wither. Deep roots are not reached by the frost.» Tolkien himself was inspired by folklore. I'd suggest returning to ancient myth, folklore, and scripture for your characters.

Alternatively, you can make your own myth. I realize that one problem our society faces today is that our culture has changed enormously from what it was even just a few hundred years ago. Sometimes old stories don't match modern values. So it can be a challenge.

However, I believe that it is far worse to allow the corporations to become our new churches than it is to use old stories. If old stories don't work for you, create your own! I believe in you and I believe that there is something inherently good and wholesome about that which comes from the heart.

The Rules of Symbolism

Powerful symbolism is a craft that takes practice. Like all crafts, there are basic dos and don'ts that those of us who practice it have learned. Here are some guidelines that will make your symbolism more powerful.

Rule 1: The Best Symbol for a Sword is a Sword

The key here is to avoid symbols of symbols. Those are weak. The more direct the symbol is, the stronger it is. This is best expressed as an example. Let's say you want a sword to represent self-discipline. A real, metal sword would be best. Next best would be, say, a letter opener in the shape of a sword. It's still metal and still has the form of a sword, only in miniature. After that, a printout from the internet of a picture of a sword.

But now let's say that, in your tradition, ferns represent swords, because their leaves resemble blades. It's fine for a fern to represent a sword, but if your goal is to represent self-discipline, that may not be your best approach. It's a symbol of a symbol: fern = sword = self-discipline. Ferns are wobbly. It's not immediately obvious what they have to do with self-discipline. You may do better with a different symbol entirely. A nail might just as easily symbolize self-discipline as a sword, for example. That's easier to come by than a sword and it's a direct symbol.

Rule 2: Concrete Trumps Abstract
Simple, direct, visceral symbols are much stronger than abstract ones. My spiritual mentor, Valerie Voigt, tells an anecdote from the 1970s. She once attended a Wiccan ritual to support the Equal Rights Amendment. The ERA was a proposed amendment to the U.S. Constitution that, had it passed, would have ensured equal rights regardless of gender. A noble goal!

The people organizing this ritual chose the actual text of the ERA for their chant. The goal was to spread the passion everyone there felt for the ERA out into the world. The problem was that the actual text is too intellectual. It doesn't go down easily into the subconscious. Valerie feels that the ritual fizzled because the legalese wasn't visceral. What was needed, Valerie felt, was something people there could really visualize. A picture, even a mental one, is worth a thousand words.

If you use a character, such as an angel, consider all the concrete attributes of that angel, not just the abstract concept it represents. Let's say you have an angel of mercy. Consider all the concrete manifestations of mercy. What does mercy look like? What would an angel of mercy hold? Maybe a sword beaten into a plowshare?

Or let's suppose you want to be more like Jesus. In addition to putting a Jesus statue on your altar, I'd encourage you to consider what specific qualities Jesus had. Reread the Gospels. Identify Jesus's teachings. A red letter Bible may help with this.

Rule 3: When in Doubt, Draw a Picture
Drawing a picture is probably one of the best ways you can make a symbol. It may sound like something out of kindergarten, but—Divinity's honest truth—the best symbols I've used spiritually have been things I drew with colored pens. I'm no artist. Stick figures

work. If you draw what you want to symbolize, it will go deep into the subconscious.

This does not contradict that the best symbol for a sword is a sword. If you have a sword, better that than a picture of one. Pictures, though, can depict things that are hard to depict in any other way. Consider depicting yourself going out into the world as a good person. You might depict a street with stores, houses, cars, and people walking by. You might depict yourself with a big huge heart in your chest and rays of kindness emanating from it to everyone else. That's difficult to depict in any other way. If you're not a skilled artist, stick figures in colored pen will work just fine.

Rule 4: Avoid Negation
Our brains have trouble negating things. Words like *no* and *not* tend to reinforce what they're negating. If I tell you not to think of an elephant, you're sure to start thinking about one. A symbol for *no smoking* will make you think of smoking.

There's another problem with negating, too. When we focus on what we don't want, we often neglect what we do want. Consider how the phrase I want everybody to not be jerks might be fulfilled by nobody communicating, because they don't want to be jerks but they don't know how to be kind.

We're responsible for being the change we want to see in the world. We're putting things out into the universe. We're an example to others. Our intentions ripple out. So be careful what you wish for. If you want everyone to be nice, as opposed to being jerks, it will be much more powerful to say I want everybody to be kinder.

A symbol of what you want to communicate to yourself is stronger than a symbol of something you don't want to communicate. Instead of no smoking, consider something like healthy lungs. If you can't think of anything else, then do as I did with this subtitle, and say avoid. Avoid smoking isn't as strong as healthy lungs, but it's still stronger than no smoking.

Rule 5: Transform Your Inner Demons
We all have inner demons: dark parts of ourselves that want to do bad things. You may be tempted to go out and look for demon images to represent vices you want to avoid. That's fine, as long as you know how to work with your inner demons. We can never get rid of any part of ourselves. Remember that "inner demon" is itself a symbol for the unethical impulses or vices within ourselves. While we cannot jettison these parts of ourselves, we *can* transform them.

Let's suppose you see anger deep within yourself. That part of you wants to lash out at anyone who makes it feel threatened. This "inner demon" cannot be banished, because it's a part of you. Attacking it will only make it stronger. Ever tried punishing yourself for being angry? If you're like me, that will only make you angrier.

You can start by listening to that inner demon, as a parent might listen to a child. Parents typically know better than children, but that doesn't mean children don't have good reasons for their emotions. Just as children need to be nurtured and guided to grow into mature adults, so do our inner demons need to be guided to grow into more functional parts of ourselves.

You may find out that your inner demon wants to hurt other people because, deep down, it's frightened. It's actually trying to protect you, but life has twisted it. What you *can* do is transform it into a guardian: a warrior that does not lash out unless it's necessary to do so.

I personally prefer the phrase "misguided inner spirit" to "inner demon".

If you get a demon figure to stand in for that inner demon, that's fine, but remember that it's a demon you plan to transform. You might want to consider that ahead of time. Maybe get two figures: a demon and a knight, for example. Replacing the demon with the knight could symbolize your misguided inner spirit transforming itself into a warrior, who will control its anger, for example.

Rule 6: Visceral Is More Powerful Than Verbal
The corollary to *concrete trumps abstract* is *visceral trumps verbal*. Words and phrases are fine, but sights, sounds, tastes, textures, smells, and anything else that appeals immediately to the senses will trump words and intellectual ideas.

Our brains are more immediately engaged. Our emotions fire faster than our thoughts, and emotions are often engaged by visceral associations. Think about toddlers. Which attracts them more: bright colors or long speeches? Whatever will turn a toddler's head will also turn an adult's more quickly than any word or phrase.

That is not to say you shouldn't use words or phrases. Words certainly have power. When you use verbal symbols, though, it's often better in poetry than prose, and better sung or chanted than just spoken. Consider the difference between these two options as ritual phrases.

1. "Now I'm going to create sacred space to help us block out the rest of the world, focus on the task at hand, and thus make our ritual more powerful."
2. "Circle! Circle! Round about!
Power stay in and world stay out!"[3]

I'll bet you think 2 is better. I agree! It has meter and rhyme. I think that makes it attractive to our inner tot, because song and poetry

---

[3] A circle casting chant invented by my spiritual mentor, Valerie Voigt, for the Waxing Moon tradition of Wicca, originaly from NROOGD.

engages us in ways prose does not. It's kind of like a dance of words.

The second phrase also follows the rule above that concrete trumps abstract. It uses concrete visuals that you can easily see in your mind. It doesn't require you to stop and think through what's being said as if you were at a college lecture. Rather, our minds immediately form visuals, and we understand the ritual act being described at a gut level.

Assembling Your Symbol Kit

I'm going to suggest that you assemble what I call your symbol kit. This will actually consist of two things: First, a written manifest of the actual symbols, and second, a collection of physical objects to serve as those symbols.

Start by writing down the symbols you think will be most useful in your pilgrimage to the Good. Then put together physical objects that represent these.

As discussed, these physical objects could be statuettes, framed printouts, even candles, scents, herbs, stones, crystals, flowers, leaves, and the like. If you already have a religion or spiritual path, you can use symbols from that, but I still think it's good to collect them, at least in your mind, so you have a good sense of what's available to you.

If you're like me, you're not very organized. (Hey! I never said I was perfect.) Fortunately, I have the luxury of being able to use my spare bedroom as a dedicated temple room (a room I do all my spiritual work in). I've worked hard to limit my chaotic non-method in that room. I store things in closets, on book shelves, in boxes hidden under altars, and wherever I can find space.

How you organize your symbols is up to you. You probably don't need a whole room. A tackle box may be useful, or a closet organizer. For some people, it's fun to look for symbols. There's nothing wrong with enjoying the journey, as long as you remember the destination and keep moving toward it.

But don't spend too, too long with this. It's easy to get bogged down in symbolism and forget our true goal: a direct experience with Goodness. If you enjoy collecting symbols, that's great, but please only spend so much time for now, because this is just the beginning. In the end, symbols are just symbols. For now, all I'll suggest is *starting* your symbol kit. It will be a lifelong process to grow it, because there are an infinite number of symbols.

To some extent, the Religion of Good is as much a spiritual art project as a devotional practice. Once you're reasonably satisfied that you have the symbols you think you're most likely to use in the Religion of Good, you're done for now.

I believe that myth transports us from the Tetrad to the Triad.

Likewise, ritual moves us from the Triad to the Dyad. In the next chapter, I'll teach you how to use your symbols in rituals that you yourself design.

6

How to Make a Ritual

I face my altar. It holds a bowl of water, a box of salt, incense in a censer, matches, a Buddhist bowl bell with a bopper, and a miniature Statue of Liberty. I hold my hand over the water: "I conjure water!" I wave my hand over the salt: "I conjure earth!" I mix three pinches of salt into the water: "Together they are the womb."[1]

I light the incense: "I conjure fire." I blow out the flame: "I conjure air. Together, they are the spark of life."[2] *I sprinkle myself and my temple room with the salt water to purify it. I wave the incense over myself and the room to bless it.*

I circle the room clockwise with my bell, ringing it with the bopper, as I chant, "Circle! Circle! Round about! Power stay in and world stay out!"[3]

I face east: "Hail to the east!" bow to the east. I turn to the right to greet and bow to the south, then the west, and then the north.

I face my statue. "Hail Lady Liberty!" I bow to her. I begin to chant, "Liberty! O, Liberty! For good and all!" I keep chanting this until I peak it.

I bow to Lady Liberty once more and thank her. I face north, then west, then south, then east, thanking each direction.

I circle the room counterclockwise, ringing the bell. "Work done! Web spun! Circle end where 'twas begun."[4] *I ring the bell one last time to end the ritual, filled with the virtue of liberty for me and for everyone.*

Welcome to the Dyad!
We move now from the world of symbols to the world of essences

---

1 These words were composed by Valerie Voigt for preparing the elements in the Esbat ritual in the Waxing Moon tradition of Wicca.
2 "Together, they are the spark of life" is my addition to the Waxing Moon tradition, for the preparation of the same elements portion of that ritual.
3 As noted earlier, these are the circle casting words of the Waxing Moon tradition, as composed by Valerie Voigt, from NROOGD.
4 These are the circle opening words for the Waxing Moon tradition's Esbat, composed by Valerie Voigt.

and abstractions. Here we find the Right-triangle-ness implied by the Pythagorean theorem. Here is the Dog-ness and Cat-ness that biologists are referring to when they give dogs and cats species names. This is the world in which the universal Platonic Form of Justice that Plato believed in resides.

I believe that the key to getting from the symbolic world of the Triad to the abstract world of the Dyad is ritual. In this chapter, I'll explain how to create your own rituals, based on the symbol kit you assembled in the previous chapter.

A ritual is really just a series of symbolic sacred acts that serve a particular purpose. What's the difference between two people being married and two people just living together? (Apart from the legal distinction, I mean.) A ritual! A wedding is a series of symbolic acts that, once completed, brings about a spiritual change between two people and a social change in terms of how they are understood by society.

We can think of a ritual as a journey that takes us from ordinary reality to sacred reality. I don't literally mean a different place, or that things that are sacred are as factual as ordinary things. Comparing ordinary reality to what I'm calling "sacred reality" is like comparing apples to oranges. Ordinary reality is a world of facts. These facts tell us a great deal about what is, but nothing about how we should feel about them. Our feelings are the realm of sacred reality.

Consider the feelings you have when you walk into a national park. When I first saw the Grand Canyon, I was filled with wonder. That's what it feels like when something is sacred to us.

I have pictures of dead relatives on my altar. Why? Someone who's purely concerned with the factual may ask what good it does to have pictures of people who are no longer here.

One answer is that I love my ancestors, and their absence does not diminish my love. Going deeper, I still relate to my memories of those loved ones, even though they're gone. In a manner of speaking, you might say that I still have an emotional relationship with them. They may be gone, but their memory lives on, and I can still relate to that memory. I can still be inspired by the wisdom they taught me or the beauty in how they lived their lives. In the factual world, they're just gone, but in the sacred world, my relationship to my memories of them lives on.

Goodness is sacred. To interact with it requires us to shift our mindset from the factual to the sacred. Ritual is one of the best ways I know of to do that. As with any craft, ritual-making has its own rules. Those of us who are expert in it have found certain wisdom about what works well and what works poorly.

The first concept I'd like to teach you is a tried-and-true structure for ritual that makes it most effective.

The Structure of Ritual
Here are the basic stages of an effective ritual.

Stage	Description
Grounding	*Anchoring yourself in ordinary reality*
Purification	*Cleansing yourself and the area*
Blessing	*Blessing yourself and the area*
Beginning Sacred Time	*Marking the beginning of the sacred work*
Creating Sacred Space	*Demarcating the place in which we will do the sacred work*
Recreating the Cosmos	*Creating a microcosm within our sacred space*
Calling on Your Characters	*Invoking appropriate characters from our symbol kit*
Doing the Work	*The core of the ritual*
Thanking Your Characters	*Allowing our symbolic characters to return to passive symbols*
Releasing the Cosmos	*Allowing the microcosm to give way to the macrocosm*
Decommissioning Sacred Space	*Allowing the space to become ordinary again*
Ending Sacred Time	*Signaling an end to our ritual*
Grounding Again	*Touching back to the world of facts*

Grounding
Before a ritual, it's important to ground ourselves in an ordinary state of mind. This is not so that we'll stay in an ordinary mental state; ideally, we want to go into an altered state of consciousness (that's what good ritual ultimately does).

Rather, it's important to be able to shift back into ordinary consciousness after the ritual is done. If we start in some sort of non-ordinary state of mind, it's easy to become detached from the mundane altogether and have trouble getting back to it. Ritual takes us up the Tetractys. It's important to know what's down in the Tetrad, so that we can return to it, because that's where we actually do good in the world.

I remember one ritual I attended at which a woman arrived three sheets to the wind. It was meant to be a ritual to help us see beyond ourselves and feel one with everybody. Now, alcohol certainly alters our consciousness and it may get us to that state. (Or not!) In this case, this woman was drunk when the ritual started, drunk during, and drunk after it ended. I can't imagine that she got much out of it.

A ritual like that only functions well when we use our insight into oneness as inspiration about how we think we ought to treat people. Arriving drunk means ending drunk, but in order to transform the momentum of the ritual into actions in real life, we need to finish sober.

To put it another way, we sometimes take a while to drift down from a ritual that really blew us out of our gourds to some vision of unity with all humanity. At some point, we need to land from that experience, sober.

Rituals allow us to transcend and sublimate mundane reality. Then when we're finished with the ritual, our state of mind returns to whatever state we had before we started. To start drunk is to finish drunk, and to finish drunk is to miss the point. It's not just that we should be sober, but our minds should be clear and down to earth so that we can be good here on earth.

Grounding techniques include anything that reminds us of the factual reality that we're departing from and that we'll return to. Touching the ground, feeling the dirt under our feet, and even just taking several deep breaths before the ritual all do this.

The technique I was trained with is a bit more elaborate. Take three deep breaths, breathing out all negativity with each breath. Close your eyes. See yourself as a tree. Extend your roots down from the base of your spine. Feel the moisture and nutrients of the earth flowing into us and filling us.

Purification

For our purposes, purification is simply the act of removing anything from our minds that we don't need in the ritual. If we're preoccupied, the ritual may very well fall flat.

Sage smudging and sprinkling holy water both accomplish this goal. When it comes to sage, I don't know enough about the religions of any Native American tribe to feel that I can give you any information on it. If you want to use holy water and believe that only priests of apostolic succession can make it, then by all means obtain holy water in whatever manner is prescribed by your religion. For those who believe that anyone can make holy water, however, I'll warn you that some occult shops take bottles with crosses on them, fill them with tap water, and sell them as "holy water" for a lot of money. If you believe you have the power to make your own holy water, I'd encourage you save your money and make it yourself.

That being said, I'm perfectly happy to share the Wiccan custom of asperging with you. We bless some salt, bless some water, and then mix them. Then we sprinkle this sacred salt water on ourselves and the space we'll use for our rituals. You don't have to be Wiccan to use it, and it doesn't imply any religious beliefs, so feel free to borrow that custom.

Blessing

Blessing is the compliment to purification. It's the act of making something sacred and bringing focus to the sacred acts we want to perform. Nature abhors a vacuum. As such, if we get rid of the negative, we should fill in the holes that are left with the positive.

In the Wicca I was taught, we accomplish this function by censing with incense. I'm happy to share this custom with you as well. Light some incense and then wave it over yourself, everyone else in the ritual, and the area in which you'll perform the ritual. You could choose an incense that has some symbolic significance for your ritual, but any will do.

Beginning Sacred Time

Sacred time is the time set aside for sacred acts, whether they are rituals, meditation, counting rosaries, or other spiritual practices.

To mark the start of sacred time, any ritual act that says *Our sacred work will now begin* will do. Some ceremonial phrase like *Let the Ritual of Goodness commence* will also work, but you need not be so grand.

I personally like ringing a bell. Remember my rule about how visceral symbols trump verbal ones? A ringing bell goes right to your inner toddler. Nothing more is needed to send the message, and you don't need to stop and think about it.

You may well ask why we ground, purify, and bless the area before creating sacred time. These first three ritual acts prepare ourselves, anyone else in the ritual, and the ritual area *before* we start sacred time and create sacred space, so that we and the area are ready for the sacred.

Creating Sacred Space

For our purposes, sacred space is simply the place you'll be performing the ritual. It's a place set aside for spiritual work.

In ancient Greece, each temple sanctuary (the sacred precinct in which the temples stood) was surrounded by a border called a *temenos*. This was sometimes a stone wall or a ditch, or sometimes natural features such as rivers or mountainsides formed parts of it. The *temenos* defined their sacred space. Similarly, you'll want to set some space aside and block out the rest of the world, so you can focus all your energy on the holy task at hand.

One way to do this is to circle the area to define the border between your sacred space and the rest of the world. In Wicca, we use special blades, called *athames*, to cut this space out from the rest of the world. However, I don't expect you to have an athame at hand, so I'll teach you a different method.

Circumambulation is just as powerful a way to define your sacred space, and it's venerable and ancient. The ancient Romans often circumambulated the areas in which they were about to perform their rituals. I suggest that you do the same. Three is a magic number, so walk three times around your space. If more than one person is in the ritual, have all participants do this.

Personally, I prefer a clockwise direction for this. Somehow, to me, clockwise movement *does* something, whereas counterclockwise movement *undoes* it. You could go counterclockwise if you prefer, though. Clockwise and the number three are just my preferences. Feel free to modify either.

If you would like to add anything to this, you could hold something in your hand. Maybe you ring a bell or shake a rattle as you go around. Maybe you sing or chant. Maybe you take incense or a candle around (but be sure to have a means of catching the candle wax). None of these are really necessary, however. Simply circumambulating is good enough.

Recreating the Cosmos

Everything we perceive is in our heads. There is a universe out there, but we only know about it through our senses.

The universe out there is the macrocosm. Our model of it in our head is the microcosm. Part of spirituality is becoming aware of this difference. Our perception of the universe is partly correct and partly incorrect. In order for us to see beyond ourselves, we must try to increase the accuracy of that perception.

One of the problems I think we humans have in knowing goodness is that we are all stuck in our own heads. We never really know other people's perspectives, not with certainty. Two people may look out on the world and see two different things, or have different sets of values about it. Goodness can only be intelligible when we get together and compare notes, because ethics is about how we treat others and how they treat us.

Many of us who design rituals have found it useful to symbolize the entire cosmos within the confines of the ritual. From there, we can—symbolically—work with anything in it. Because this will be informed by our understanding of the cosmos, this symbolic cosmos will come primarily from our microcosm. However, as we practice more and more, we'll likely want to try to touch the macrocosm. As we gain more insight into it, we'll want to change our own microcosm. By symbolizing the cosmos, we create the opportunity for this work to take place.

We can do this by making the sacred space be a symbolic universe. When we understand it this way, our ritual acts become symbolic acts within ourselves, within our microcosm. The ritual becomes a model of our understanding of reality, which we can then interact with to try to gain insight. In our case, that insight is into goodness, which entails relationships between us and others.

There are several ways to ritually symbolize the cosmos. In Wicca, we call upon the four directions in a ritual act called Quarter Calling. In many forms of Wicca, we also include the four elements—fire, water, earth, and air—in this.[5] To Call the Quarters, a Wiccan faces each cardinal direction and says some words about that direction and possibly the element associated with it.

Some Wiccans include up, down, and center, as well. I won't go into detail about this here, because this isn't a book on Wicca. For your ritual, you could face each cardinal direction and salute it in some fashion and then salute up, down, and center. We Wiccans often start with East, because that's where the sun rises and the sun has special significance for us, but you could do it in whatever order makes sense to you. There are other approaches as well. You could simply salute sky and earth. I also know some people who salute sky, earth, and sea.

Calling on Your Characters

Choose which characters you'll use from the symbol kit you assembled in the last chapter. The next step in your ritual will be to call on them. Even if you don't believe in them literally, we want to take them seriously as symbols. Let's treat them almost as if they're real (but don't go wild with this). I don't mean that you should invent an imaginary friend—that's too much. I do think it's nice to be polite to such beings, even if they are just in our imagination. We're trying to be good, after all, so let's practice on our characters.

Let's say we've decided to work with Athena, from Greek mythology. Rather than saying *Hey! Athy! Get over here!*, it's more appropriate in that sense to say something formal and majestic, such as *I call*

---

[5] To reassure readers who are more scientifically minded: Most Wiccans I know are well aware of the periodic table. When we talk about *the four elements*, we're referring not to literal elements but to a rich body of symbolism that has come down to us. Likewise, we realize that the cardinal directions only seem to exist on our planet, but that you can't really go north or south any further than the poles and that east and west just take you around the globe, not off into space. We know we're working symbolically. Calling the Quarters works for me, because we experience life on earth in terms of four directions.

upon the great Goddess Athena!

I've also found that it's a good idea to insert something about them, to remind us why we're calling on them. Epithets work really well, because they specify *why* we're using a character as a symbol. If we're using Athena as a symbol for wisdom, we might say, *I call upon Wise Athena! Please help me be wise, so I can be my best self.*

Write a call for each character you want to work with. I think it's best if they follow the same rough pattern each time. This goes something like this: *I call upon (attribute) (character)! Help me (what you want help with).* Vary this as you need to. For example, *I call upon Michael, Archangel of Self-Discipline! Please help me master myself.*

Using this technique forms a pattern in our minds that I think our subconsciouses can relate to more easily.

Doing the Work

This is the section of the ritual where you accomplish its main purpose. Everything leading up to it sets the scene, as it were. You've grounded, you've purified the space, you've established sacred space and time, you've symbolized the cosmos, you've invited your characters to join you. Now you do the most important part: performing the actual goal of the ritual.

Whole books could be written on how to accomplish this, so please forgive my mysteriousness for now. Since this is a chapter on ritual, let me talk generally about what goes here and then fill it in in more detail in just a bit. This is the most art-project-like part of the whole ritual process. One of my favorite options, which I mentioned in the last chapter, is drawing a picture of what you want to symbolize. Again, stick figures are fine.

If you have more people, a symbolic drama can work too, but it takes a lot of rehearsing and coordination. Several people could dress up as the characters and everyone else could go to various stations, where each character imparts something to them. Maybe you start on one side of the room with the Angel of Severity, holding a sword. Then you go to the other end of the room to meet the Angel of Mercy with a heart over her chest, to indicate compassion. Then, you'd go to the center to meet Justice, holding the scales of balance between severity and mercy. At each station, the character would give you a little speech about it.

A third possibility, which I also think is great when done by yourself, is to come up with a chant or mantra you can recite over and over again. If you want to boost your self-esteem about your ability to be good, you might sing the chorus of that old gospel song, *This little light of mine, I'm gonna let it shine! Let it shine! Let it shine! Let it shine!* After several repetitions, you might transition to just repeating *Let it shine! Let it shine! Let it shine!* over and over again. When designing this part, it's a good idea to reread my rules for symbolism in the previous chapter. They'll guide you in the dos and don'ts.

In the next chapter, I'll teach you how to do the ecstatic part, so that you can get out of your gourd and come to some vision or insight into unity, and thence to get a handle on the Good. Once you've learned how to do that, that ecstatic experience will go here, in the middle of the ritual.

For now, though, insert the ritual act that symbolizes the main thing you want to accomplish here. This is sort of like the ritual within the ritual. This could be singing, dancing, chanting, or the like. It could also be something that interacts with your characters. For example, if you have scales on your altar to symbolize Justice, and the goal of your ritual is to make sure your sense of justice is balanced within yourself, you might set the scales up unbalanced *before* the ritual and then balance them as the ritual act in this central section.

Thanking Your Characters

Once you're done with the main work, you bring the ritual to an end, through a series of steps similar to the ones you took to set it up.

The first of these is to thank the characters you "invited." Speaking of mercy and severity, my Wiccan teacher, Valerie, is merciful with students performing rituals—except in just one instance in which she is totally severe. *Don't dismiss the Gods!* she's always telling us. For one thing, it's arrogant of us to dismiss them. More importantly, the Gods are cosmic beings who are always everywhere and ever with us. To dismiss a deity of agriculture, for example, is to symbolically wish blight on the earth. Any ritual meant to bring us prosperity will have bad symbolism if prosperity itself is banished at the end.

I know we're just using characters as symbols, here, though many in Wicca really believe in the Gods.[6] And of course, as mere symbols, our characters can't be offended. Still, if we want to hone our art of symbolic ritual, we should pay careful attention to how we use our symbols. Even if our angels, heroes, and storybook characters are just symbols, dismissing them becomes a symbol of rudeness. To practice rudeness in a ritual meant to elevate our virtues symbolically negates exactly what we are trying to nurture in ourselves. If we want more compassion, for example, dismissing the Angel of Compassion has the symbolic effect of getting rid of the very compassion we're trying to cultivate in ourselves.

Instead, I like to thank my characters with words like *George Washington the Honest, thank you for your attention and for your blessing in*

---

[6] Wicca is defined by practice rather than belief. We don't have to believe anything. Many Wiccans *don't* believe literally in our divinities and still *do* work with them in more symbolic ways. I'm just pointing out that you don't have to believe in supernatural beings to work with characters this way.

this rite. You are with me always. We thank our characters to signal the end of their involvement in the ritual. Giving thanks to an unreal being still involves our feelings of gratitude. This ritual act brings our involvement with the character to a close, at least for the purposes of the ritual we're currently performing. It also reinforces the virtue we are trying to cultivate by thanking the personification of that virtue.

Releasing the Cosmos
At this point in the ritual, we undo what we did in Recreating the Cosmos. It was important to us to have a model of the cosmos available in the ritual. However, as we wind down, it's equally important to let that model go, precisely so that we can return to reality, which no model perfectly reflects.

In Wicca, we perform the ritual act known as Dismissing the Quarters. We face each direction again, thank it, and then dismiss it. We understand each quarter guardian (the spirit of each direction and element) as withdrawing from the edge of our circle (our sacred space) to the edge of the cosmos. In some Wiccan traditions, we do this in the same order as we called each quarter. In others, we dismiss quarters in reverse order. While there are Wiccan justifications for each, for our purposes the two are equivalent.

If you called on the four directions, up, down, and center, for example, feel that all but center are withdrawing to the edge of the cosmos. Since every point in the universe is the center of it, the center doesn't go anywhere—but it does change from being the center of your sacred space to being a center of the cosmos. (Remember, every point is the center of the cosmos).

Decommissioning Sacred Space
The next step is to allow the sacred space you created earlier to become an ordinary part of the world again. This tells us that we are no longer using the space for a sacred purpose, and we are just allowing it to go back to being mundane.

In Wicca, we do this through a ritual act known as Opening Circle, in which we take the athame back around a second time. What I recommend to you is to circumambulate in the reverse of whichever direction you circumambulated before. Earlier, I recommended that you create sacred space through clockwise movement, so here I recommend counterclockwise movement to decommission sacred space. But it's up to you.

Ending Sacred Time
In order to signal that the ritual is at an end, repeat whatever you did at the beginning to start sacred time, or something comparable. If you rang a bell, ring it again. If you said *Let the ritual commence,* say

something equivalent such as *Thus, the ritual is complete.*

Grounding Again
Just as we should start grounded and fully aware of ordinary reality before a ritual, we should ground afterward as well. One possibility is to repeat the tree visualization that I gave earlier. Some people touch their brows to the floor. This can double as a final devotional act, worshiping Goodness (and God, if you believe in God).

It's also good to allow the effects of the ritual to percolate. There's a balance here, which I'll discuss in more detail later in the chapter. The key is to let things flow, without overthinking it. Often, one of the best ways to ground is with a meal and some light conversation. Allow yourself to be back in ordinary reality. The effects are already taking place within you.

Rules of Ritual
Just as there is conventional wisdom I've learned about symbolism, which I shared with you in the last chapter, there are dos and don'ts with ritual. Experience has shown that certain techniques work better than others.

Some people may use this book for solo practice, while others may get together in small circles of peers to work through it together. I've provided some guidelines below for both group and solo rituals, since I think I owe it to my readers to give guidance on both.

(I have also included more information about working in a group in Appendix III. You may find this information useful even if you're just working solo.)

Rule 1: Plan Your Ritual Beforehand
You don't necessarily need to spend hours or days planning out every single ritual, but you should figure out what you're going to do before you do it, applying the rules of symbolism from the last chapter and these rules here. Planning out your ritual helps it be its best. Think through your symbolism, work on your chants, and figure out all the steps you'll take.

I highly recommend that you make a checklist of everything you'll need, and check it off twice. The first time is to make sure you have what's needed for the ritual, like a Buddha statue or some frankincense incense. The second time is to make sure you've covered all your bases for the ritual (check off how you'll create sacred space, for example). As you get better at it, you may be able do this all in your head. Even after over twenty years of ritual design, though, I still plan things out.

If more than one person is involved, make sure they know what's planned and that they're participating in getting everything together. Rehearsals are a must for any group ritual. Without rehearsals, your ritual will likely resemble a first grade Christmas or Chanukah pageant. Properly rehearsed, though, it may move you to tears, and I'd love for you to be moved to tears.

They say that art is 10% inspiration and 90% perspiration. This preparation time is the perspiration part. It may not be fun, but your ritual will be much, much more successful if you take the time.

Rule 2: Be Passionate
Be positively passionate about spiritual work. If you're ready to start your ritual, it's critical that your entire being buy into what you're doing.

Of course, if you wait until you have no reservations whatsoever, you'll never perform the ritual. The point is that your mind, heart, and soul should all be fully committed. If you're not actively passionate, I'd suggest that you find out what's wrong and fix it first. Otherwise, the ritual may well fall flat.

If you're working with a group, make sure everyone is passionate. If they're not, fix it. You don't have to agree on absolutely every detail.[7] Compromise is a must for group work. However, if someone has reservations or is even lukewarm about it, it may cause the ritual to fizzle.

I once had a woman come to my Wiccan circle. As we were discussing the ritual we were all there to do, she said that she didn't care how we did it. I know that some people are just shy or else don't want to rock the boat, so I explained to her about how important passion is. She refused to express any passion about what we had planned and wouldn't tell us why. She also wouldn't tell us what she *was* passionate to do. It seemed she wasn't passionate to do anything, but she'd go along with whatever we did.

Since she said she was fine with everything, we went ahead with the ritual, but it ended up being weak. Some people just like doing rituals, but that's not a good enough reason to do them. Other people have private reservations about certain things, but can be passive in expressing them. If that's you, you should be assertive enough that your group knows you're uncomfortable. Group work is an art in and of itself, which I'll come back to in the appendices. Checking in with your group is all important. If someone's not totally committed, they don't need to tell everyone else why, but the group should work

---

[7] One important tip in ritual by committee, however, is make sure everyone knows, at a high level, the entire ritual. I've known rituals by committee that were disasters, because they assigned each person a role and invited each person to do things their own way without consulting the rest of the group. They just showed up on the day of the ritual, everybody doing their own thing, only to find that the whole thing fizzled because there was too much chaos. Having everyone on the same page is a must.

together to find something everyone *is* passionate about.

The same need for passion applies even if you're practicing alone. There's a sense in which you're still a group, even if it's just a group of one. You're both the performer/officiator of the ritual and the audience/participant. We still want to engage ourselves in what we're doing, if we hope to get up the Tetractys to gain perspective on the Good. It's important for the officiants of a group ritual to engage the audience, and that advice will mostly hold true as well for solo practice. If all goes well, the part of yourself that is participating in the ritual will be enthralled by the part of yourself that's officiating it.

Rule 3: Project Your Voice!
This usually only pertains to group rituals, and then only when you don't need to worry about disturbing the neighbors. If it's just you alone, or you know your group needs to be quiet, this advice doesn't apply to you.

In all other cases, though, everyone participating in the ritual should be sure to project their voices. They shouldn't yell, but they should be heard clearly across the sacred space. If you imagine your voice traveling to everyone's ears, and you let your voice rise to the volume you imagine is needed to do that, everyone will probably hear you without your needing to strain your voice or yell. The result is a nice, resonant voice that has majesty.

I remember one time when I attended a Wiccan Sabbat (a seasonal holiday), just as a congregant rather than as an officiant. The Gods had been thanked. The quarters were dismissed. The circle had been opened. The candles snuffed. It looked to most of us, including me, like it was over. The priest was saying something, but, forty feet across the circle, I couldn't hear.

Several people had started talking about us all adjourning to the potluck, which was to take place afterward. Suddenly, the priest and several officiants were angrily shushing everybody. Those of us on my end of the room were baffled. In the end, we found out that the priest wanted us to all hold hands and say a final prayer, but many of us couldn't hear the request. We eventually came to order, but it ruined the moment.

The lesson here is that it's on the officiants of a ritual to make themselves heard. If people don't know what you want them to do, all the majesty of the ritual will disappear.

Rule 4: Be Dramatic
Even if you're just performing your ritual on your own, good drama engages us. Anything prosaic bores us.

Some think that people should be so self-disciplined, so in control of their own powers of concentration, that they will stay tuned in even to the most prosaic speech. If you're one of these people, then I'll agree with you that self-discipline is a good virtue—but then I encourage you to be more practical and realize that expecting everyone to be able to listen to prosaic speech for any length of time without their attention wandering goes against human nature.

If you have lines or a chant, speak them with gusto. If you need to keep your voice down so as not to wake your neighbors or housemates, use a stage whisper. If you speak dramatically, but lower the volume of your voice, it will still come across with power.

Imagine your words coming out of your mouth and resounding through the cosmos, even while speaking softly. Speak slowly and deliberately enough to be heard, even if you're by yourself—it's important for you to hear yourself, too.

Even if you're by yourself, don't just think the words. Speak them out loud, even if only in a whisper. Thoughts are too dreamy and wispy; we engage with spoken words much better.

If you have actions to take, make them big (but don't burn the house down because you struck your match with too much panache). Grand gestures engage us. You want everyone attending, including you, to be engaged.

Depending on how much work you want to put in, it may help to dress up, put on masks, and do anything else that will heighten the drama. Even if it's just you, there's something about dressing up that brings out our inner thespian. If being dramatic is difficult for you, keep practicing. I was shy when I started, and it was hard for me to be loud and dramatic. It helped me, though, to understand that what I was doing was a service for everyone in attendance, including myself. When I realized that I was helping people, rather than performing before critics, it reframed what I was doing in terms of duty.

Rule 5: The Show Must Go On

We all have rituals that go off script, as it were. When that happens, the best thing to do is roll with it. It's a spiritual ritual, not Shakespeare. There are no critics to write bad reviews if you get your lines wrong. If it's just you, there's no one else to criticize you. If it's for a group, they won't know you went off script.

The most important thing is that you keep the majesty and power of the ritual going. If you stop and shuffle papers or whisper to a colleague or look something up in a book, all that majesty and power will grind to a halt. People will notice when that happens—but if you start improvising and you keep things going, they'll never know anything was wrong.

Even if the ritual is just for you, isn't nature more beautiful than any work of art? Isn't your impromptu inspiration more beautiful than you putting things on hold while you try to get back on script?

In fact, it's when we have no one else to perform for that we most easily forget that we're still performing for a very important audience: ourselves. Stopping to "stay on script" will cause your inner toddler to get bored. Continuing with passion will keep your whole being engaged.

Climbing the Tetractys to meet the Good face to face is important. It will help you gain ethical intuition. It's kind of like riding a bike: You have to keep going or you'll fall.

But you got this. Just as you learned to keep your balance on a bike and guide where it goes, you can guide your ritual.

If you can't figure out what happens next, just make something up. Remember when I said that it's important for you to be positively passionate about what the ritual before you start? Well, now is the time to harness that passion. What's the worst that could happen? Your lines don't make sense? Hey, some of my favorite songs are by the Beatles and Led Zeppelin, but I never did figure out what "I Am the Walrus" and "Stairway to Heaven" were about.

Who cares? They rock! More importantly, they speak to our hearts poetically.

Rule 6: Engage Everyone

If you're performing the ritual as part of a group, it's important to engage everyone rather than allow them to be passive observers. Let them participate and put energy (so to speak) into the proceedings.

One of the easiest ways to do this is to have a simple chant that you'll all speak together. I like to use chants that are so simple that people can join in after a few repetitions. Start the chant yourself, and then motion with your hands to invite them to join in. Most people will figure it out and start chanting. If done right, you won't need to teach people anything ahead of time. It will flow naturally.

Another approach to this is call-and-response. Chant one line and have them repeat it. Then chant the next one and have them repeat that. You can just say *This is call and response* before the chant and most people will get it.

Of course, if you're working solo, you don't need call and response or to make sure everybody's engaged, because everybody's just you. But you should still make sure the ritual will engage you.

Rule 7: Use Humor Appropriately

This rule primarily applies to group rituals. I've never believed in stuffy rituals. Rituals should be exuberant. When people are worried they have to follow a bunch of rules, they disengage.

However, there's a balance here. Too much silliness and people won't take it seriously. We're using rituals for serious purposes, so ultimately we want people to take them seriously.

I believe that about ninety percent of a ritual should be serious. If you perform it with elegance and solemnity, it will move people. However, it's great to inject humor maybe ten percent of the time. The goal of this is simply to let people know they don't have to be stuffy. Get them to relax. Then get on with the majesty of your ritual, and that will impart seriousness.

Something to be aware of is what psychologists call the flow state. This state comes about when your mind is so engaged with the task at hand that you aren't thinking about anything else. In this state, the mind stills. This is a powerful tool to spiral up, as it were, spiritually.

Too much solemnity and too much levity can both be problems. Too much levity allows ritual details to slide and gives the mind other things to focus on, which can bring people out of the flow state. But too much solemnity can give the mind more to pay attention to than it is capable of, which also causes people to disengage.

You should probably be clear in your mind whether one of the goals of your ritual is to achieve the flow state. If it's not, than you have one less thing to worry about. If it is, and it's just by yourself, it's easy. Try to make things just complicated enough to occupy your mind, but not so much that you get overwhelmed.

The problem with trying to achieve flow states in the minds of many people at a public event is that everyone's minds will be filled to capacity at different points. Consider that the better you know a ritual, the more elaborate it will need to be to fully occupy your mind. But others won't know the ritual that you've rehearsed, so their minds will be more easily occupied by its demands.

Unless everyone in the ritual has rehearsed it together, I recommend *not* trying to perform a ritual that is so perfect that everyone's minds will go into the flow state. If you're a member of a group that is trying to collectively enter into a flow state, being formal about ritual may well be important, since the goal is for everybody to be doing a particular thing at a particular time. But in rituals where the flow state is less important, it matters much less whether each act is done just so. Still, striking a balance between getting people to loosen up and not be too stuffy versus getting people to be appropriately serious is your best bet.

I once officiated a memorial service for a dearly departed Wiccan woman who had atheist friends. Knowing nothing of Wicca, they sat very quietly and respectfully, as if in church, and participated very little, even when encouraged to. I realized they were too worried they'd make a mistake.

Fortunately, one of the candles we had put on the altar was duck-shaped. This was to honor the Great Duck, since our dearly departed had been a member of a coven known as Daughters of the Duck.

I called on the Goddess and God of Wicca with great solemnity.

Then I called on Duck, lit the candle, and said, *Quack!* All smiles, the atheists chorused, *Quack!* Now they had license to loosen up.

After that, I went back to the solemnity that befits a memorial service. They proceeded to participate with reverence, enabled by just a bit of levity. To quote from Lao Tzu's *Tao Te Ching*, "Thoughtless people hear about the Tao and make jokes about it. It wouldn't be the Tao if there weren't jokes about it."

Rule 8: The Twenty-Four Hour Rule
In Wicca, the Witch's Pyramid is a concept that describes four key ingredients necessary for good ritual: to know, to will, to dare, and to keep silent. In the Waxing Moon tradition we teach "keep silent" as the twenty-four hour rule.

In order to give the effects of a spiritual practice time to percolate through us, it's best to keep quiet about it. If we talk about it, write about it, or post about it on social media, it can lead us to over-intellectualize what we've done. This can unravel it. We wonder whether our mind has really changed, so of course it doesn't. It's a self-fulfilling prophecy.

Since it's all happening within us, it's really our decision whether or not a spiritual act is profound and life-changing. The twenty-four hour rule holds that it takes twenty-four hours for the percolation to take place. Avoid talking or writing about what you've done for twenty-four hours.

The best way to turn your thoughts elsewhere is to keep your mind occupied with other things. Work, play, get together with friends, laugh, love, go for a walk in nature. All these things will help the work percolate in the background.

Above all, let go of any worry about thinking about it. Remember the "don't think of an elephant" trap. If you try too hard to stop thinking about it, you'll think about it. Let go and get on with life for twenty-four hours instead.

Sample Ritual Template
Here's a ritual template you can use. Some of this ritual comes from the Waxing Moon tradition of Wicca. Some of this also comes from what I think will be most beneficial to you. For example, I've changed using an athame for circle casting to circumambulation, since I don't expect you to own a athame if you're not Wiccan.

Ritual design is like cooking. At first you learn out of cookbooks. Then you experiment with modifying recipes. Then you make your own recipes from scratch. In the end, it's a matter of tasting what's good. If you're new to ritual, you might think of this as one of the first recipes in your cookbook. Or if you've already started your collection of rituals, then here's another one to add to it.

80   *The Religion of Good*

This particular ritual is about liberty. I've made that the focus of my sample because I assume that all of us living in a free society can agree on this value. However, if you'd like to focus on a different virtue, please feel free to change it. My goal for now is just to provide you with an example of how a ritual might look using the structure and techniques I've suggested. As with all the rituals in this book, I've also put this in Appendix I—but without all the explication, to make it easier to use as an outline while actually performing the ritual.

Note that everything in this book's rituals is merely symbolic, even when I don't say that explicitly. The ritual below is meant to bless us with the virtue of liberty. With liberty comes responsibility. Let's use our freedom for good purposes.

Preparation

Set the following things on an altar. This could be any table or surface. Beforehand, you may want to drape a colorful cloth over this to decorate it. Here's what you'll need:
1. A bowl of water
2. A container of salt
3. A censer (incense holder) to burn incense
4. Incense in the censer
5. Matches or a lighter to light the incense
6. A bell[8]
7. Optionally, a fan to fan the incense
8. A small replica or image of the Statue of Liberty.[9]

Grounding

1. Sit or stand comfortably.
2. Take three deep breaths. With each breath, breath in cosmic energy, hold for a moment, then breath negative emotions into the earth. You can pick up your negative emotions afterward the ritual, if you still need them.
3. Feel that you are a tree.
4. Send your roots deep down into the earth.
5. Draw up the moisture, nutrients, and power of Mother Earth.
6. Feel it rise up your spine.
7. Reach your fingers up above your head, like branches.
8. Say, **I am here. I am here. I am here.**

---

[8] I prefer Buddhist bowl-shaped bells, because you can ring them with a baton, rather than bells that have their own knockers in them. That way, I can ring the bell precisely as many times as I intend, rather than have the knocker ring it several more times than I meant to. But you can use whatever works, or even just clap your hands, instead.
[9] A printout from the internet will do.

Purification
1. Touch your hand to the bowl and say, **I conjure water.**
2. Touch your hand to the salt container and say, **I conjure earth.**
3. Take three pinches of salt and mix it with the water in the bowl, saying, **Together, they are the womb.**
4. Sprinkle yourself, anyone else in the ritual, and the space with the salt water, working your way around the room clockwise. If you have anything in the room that shouldn't get wet, you may want to just go through the motions, without actually sprinkling water on it.
5. As you sprinkle, visualize moonlight clearing away all negativity.

Blessing
1. Light the incense. Say, **I conjure fire! I conjure air! Together, they are the spark of life.**
2. Pick up the censer and the fan, if you're using one.
3. Fan or wave the incense smoke over you, anyone else in the ritual, and the space in which you're holding the ritual, again moving clockwise around the space.
4. As you do, visualize sunlight blessing the area with goodness.

Beginning Sacred Time and Creating Sacred Space
1. Walk around the ritual area three times, ringing the bell. Ringing the bell indicates the beginning of sacred time. Circumambulating defines sacred space.
2. As you do so, chant, **Circle! Circle! Round about! Power stay in and world stay out!**
3. When you come back to the altar, ring the bell one more time, before setting it back down.

Recreating the Cosmos
1. Face east and say, **Hail to the spirits of the east.** If you prefer, you can say *angels* instead of *spirits*.
2. Repeat this for **south, west,** and **north,** so that you salute each direction clockwise from east to north.

Call on Lady Liberty
1. If you are performing the ritual with others, stand in a circle and join hands. If by yourself, face the Statue of Liberty on your altar.
2. Say, **Lady Liberty! Praise be to thee! Help us take responsibility for our freedom. Help us grow from individuals to citizens, from citizens to cosmopolitans, each ready to steer the Ship of State.**
3. Bow.

Doing the Work
1. If you are working with others, hold hands in a circle. Otherwise, stand in front of the altar, facing the center of the area.
2. Start chanting, **Freedom! O, freedom! For good and for all!**
3. Continue to chant as you dance clockwise in a circle. If you can't dance due to disability or the like, just sit or stand and chant. If you're in a group and one or more of your members is too disabled to dance, invite them to sit and provide them with a chair and a rhythm instrument to play during the dance; if you don't have an instrument, invite them to clap. Also, some people have trouble chanting and dancing at the same time. If that's you, just chanting is perfectly fine.
4. Keep chanting and dancing until you feel you're done, perhaps three to seven rounds, or several minutes.
5. If you know you won't disturb anybody with the noise, give a big whoop or ululation at the end to really shoot off your chant like fireworks on the Fourth of July.

Thanking Lady Liberty
1. Once again join hands, if in a group, or face your Statue of Liberty, if it's just you.
2. Say, **Lady Liberty. Thank you for your attention and your blessing in this rite. You are with us always.**

Releasing the Cosmos
1. Face north. Say, **North! Thank you for your blessing on this rite. Farewell!**
2. Do the same for **west, south**, and **east**, saying farewell to each direction counterclockwise.

Decommissioning Sacred Space and Ending Sacred Time
1. Walk counterclockwise around the ritual area three times, ringing the bell.
2. As you do so, chant, **Work done! Web spun! Circle end where 'twas begun.**
3. When you return to the altar, ring the bell one last time before setting it down.

Grounding Again
1. Kneel down.
2. Touch your head to the ground.
3. Feel any remaining "energy" from the ritual go into the earth.
4. After the ritual, I suggest doing something fun, enjoying your freedom.

Suggested Reading

The two best books on ritual design, in my not so humble opinion, are *Neopagan Rites* and *Real Magic*, both by Isaac Bonewits. Despite the title, *Neopagan Rites* is not just for Neopagans. While targeted to Neopagans (Wicca is one of the Neopagan religions), the entire book is about how to perform successful rituals. It's accessible to all religions.

Real Magic is Bonewits's book on "magic". Well, a lot of us Wiccans believe in magic, by some definition.[10] And, hey, Christians believe in resurrection, which is cool by me. I think all religions have strange ideas, and mine is no exception.

Bonewits has some unusual beliefs of his own that you may not hold with, such as psychic abilities. That's okay. If you change every place he says *magic* to *symbolic ritual act* and change *magic ritual* to *symbolic ritual*, you may find that what he says becomes more useful to you. In this way, you can easily jettison his beliefs and use the book as a practical guide to effective ritual.

What's good about *Real Magic* is that Bonewits breaks down, in a deep way, how ritual symbolism works. It's valuable information for us. While *Neopagan Rites* is about the general template of a ritual, *Real Magic* will give you a lot of information on how to really ramp up that mysterious main portion into high gear.

Not everybody likes Bonewits's style. He can be snarky and often comes across as contemptuous of mainstream religion. This comes out most in *Real Magic*, since he was quite the 1970s young radical when he wrote it. By the time he was writing *Neopagan Rites*, he'd settled down—*a bit*. I don't take his sharp wit too seriously, and I tend to find it a welcome relief from old, stuffy books on religion, but he's not for everyone. If you can tolerate his style, he has a lot to teach about effective ritual.

Perform a Ritual

Now it's your turn. I invite you to design and perform your own ritual.

I suggest that it be just for you. If you're reading this book with a group of people, and you'd like to do something together, by all means do so. Just remember that it's easier to learn if you practice just on your own first. If you're shy, one plus to starting out by yourself is that there's no one to be self-conscious in front of. Don't worry if you make mistakes. Remember that the show must go on.

If you want, you can start with the sample ritual I have above, or you can modify it to suit the needs of your religion. You can also write your own, based on the guidelines I've given in this chapter.

---

10 I personally understand magic more in terms of mysterious power than supernatural power.

Use the symbol kit you developed.

What I'd like you to start doing is getting in the habit of designing and performing rituals. Symbolic ritual is really at the heart of the Religion of Good. Our goal is to "worship" Goodness, as it were. Ritual is the place we will worship within and the launchpad from which we will finally reach the escape velocity we need to have a direct experience of the Good. In the next chapter, I'll discuss the third and final component to all this, which is the ecstasy of direct experience.

7
Direct Experience of the Good

I sit on a meditation cushion in my temple room. My front door is locked. I've already grounded, purified, and blessed myself and my temple room, created sacred space, called the quarters, and called on the Source of All Things—the genderless and impersonal highest divinity in my form of Wicca—to help me in my work.

In front of me is a Buddhist bowl bell. I ring it. Its sound causes my rational mind to recede. I begin to chant as the tone of the bell slowly fades. "I am we! We are one! One are we! And we am I!" The meaning of the words fades, until only the sound is left. I nod with the chant. I begin to go into an ecstatic state. All the symbolism and ritual forms my trajectory. It programs my inner autopilot to take me to the Good.

Welcome to the Monad!
Well... not quite yet. The Monad is a beautiful city in a hidden valley where all is one. It's ineffable and mysterious. Words fail to describe it, and this is a book of words, so words are already failing me.

Yet it's a perspective you must attain in order to glimpse the Good, because ethics is about all of us together.[1] "When you've seen beyond yourself, then you may find that peace of mind is waiting there," sayeth the Beatles. You need an ecstatic experience to get you there. Singing, chanting, dancing, or drumming will all do.

But not any ecstatic experience will do. It must be one within a ritual, which is informed by symbolism, which symbolizes your understanding of goodness. Going to your local drum circle will probably get you out of your gourd, but it won't necessarily be tied into your symbolism of goodness. (But drum circles are good in and of

---

[1] Following the path I've laid out, anyway. There are multiple approaches to the ethics crisis, and I don't mean to dismiss others. But if we're going to follow the approach I'm recommending, which is the path up the Tetractys and back down again, then gaining some sort of perspective on the unity of All is essential, however fleeting or nebulous that may be at first.

themselves, so by all means go!) Without the right context, it's a little like parachuting over Hawaii: You'll land somewhere, but it might not be Waikiki.

I believe that mythic or scriptural symbolism gets us from the mundane Tetrad to the symbolic Triad. Ritual gets us from there to the abstract Dyad. To get from there to the absolute Monad, we need to have an experience of getting beyond ourselves.

One reason why I think we have so much trouble thinking through ethics, in modern times, is that we're in ourselves all the time. That's good in many ways. We are individuals in a free society, and that's as it should be.[2] However, in this state, we're left with trying to find ethics in a cold cosmos. Nature does not seem to tell us how we *ought* to act.[3]

I believe that to be ethical requires us to try to experience all of us as one, perhaps even all of the universe as one. From that perspective, we can experience goodness directly. To do that, we have to get out of our heads. And to do that, we'll need an ecstatic experience.

Even then, when we have one, we'll only *glimpse* the Good. Because we're imperfect beings, we will never know it perfectly. Still, that glimpse makes all the difference.

An ecstatic experience is anything that helps you see beyond yourself to something greater. Anyone who's ever gone to church, synagogue, or some other place of worship and been caught up in the ecstasy of God (or the Divine or the Sacred) knows what I'm talking about. Choir music, drumming, dancing, chanting, and singing have all been used by many cultures across history to accomplish this. Everyone does this a bit differently, so you should pick a method that works well for you.

So what is an ecstatic experience? Ecstatic experiences allow our brains to stop being so rational, stop thinking quite so much, stop processing emotions quite so intensely, and to let go of focusing on us and our lives. They allow us instead to let go of focus altogether and allow our minds to become temporarily unfocused.

Focus is a virtue, but transcendence is another. Balance is dynamic.

---

[2] For a fuller unpacking of this, see my Appendix IV on ethics in a free society. There I remind us that, while we are indeed individuals, we are also citizens of all the free societies we're members of, as well as cosmopolitans (citizens of the world) and have duties as well as rights, as such.

[3] Many will point out that we can learn ethics from nature. I don't see this as really contradicting a perspective that understands the cosmos as essentially amoral, though. I don't see the cosmos as intentionally providing us with some sort of God-given morality in the way that I think Kant, for one, hoped we would. That does not in any way preclude us from, say, observing how other species cooperate or recognizing that cooperation is a powerful survival strategy or that wisdom might include such ideas as war is typically foolish or that worldwide cooperation may be an even better survival strategy, if it can be achieved, than cooperation only within smaller social units. "The Tao ... is an eternal void, filled with infinite possibilities." (Lao Tzu, *Tao Te Ching*, Chapter 4)

Direct Experience of the Good   87

Balancing virtues sometimes means emphasizing one at some times and emphasizing another at others. We need focus for ordinary life, and there are other times and places in which reason is useful, but we need transcendence to glimpse the Good. In order to achieve that transcendence, we need ecstatic experiences.

This lack of focus can take us to various vague areas in the terrain of our consciousness, but we want it to take us to one particular type of non-focus in which we feel our connectedness to all humanity, all sentient life, even the whole cosmos. All our symbolism and ritual will preprogram our brain, as it were, with the right flight path to take us there. Our ecstatic experience, however, must allow ourselves eventually to go on autopilot. To get to the Good requires a leap of faith.

This type of consciousness is sometimes described as a type of trance, but a trance is nothing to worry about. The movies and TV have used trances and hypnotism in their plots as though hypnotists can control people's minds, and once you're in a trance, you can never break out of it, unless you have psychic powers or something. Hogwash!

In fact, anyone who's ever gone to a hypnotherapist will tell you that hypnosis is voluntary and you can snap out of it whenever you want to. Why do stage hypnotists get people to act like chickens? Because their subjects are there to be entertained and to entertain; they actually want to be hypnotized into acting like chickens or they wouldn't have volunteered. (Either that or they are shills collaborating with the hypnotist.)

That being said, it *is* valid to worry about trance in the context of dangerous cults. There are spiritual fakes out there who want to control you, not to put on a basically honest show and include you in the joke, but because they've learned to manipulate their fellow human beings for their own unethical purposes. The key is to realize that dangerous cults pervert the techniques of honest religions and spirituality in order to control people. Those techniques can include pseudo-ecstatic experiences that are part of brainwashing. I say *pseudo* because true transcendent experiences cause us to rise above these sort of cultish ideologies and liberate ourselves from those who try to control us. How to resist dangerous cults is way beyond the scope of this book and my own expertise. Suffice it to say that there are legitimate uses of spiritual techniques, and that's what I'm advocating.[4]

---

[4] It's unfortunate that I'm stuck using the word *cult* here. To the ancient Greco-Romans, *cult* referred simply to the body of religiosity around a particular deity or set of deities, and the word is still used that way by classicists and other scholars of antiquity. By that definition, it should not be at all offensive to describe Christianity, for example, as the Christ cult, or Judaism as the Yahweh cult. Unfortunately, Christendom has historically used *cult* to describe both the dangerous pseudo-spiritualities that seek to manipulate people, which I'm referring to here,

When I talk about ecstatic experiences, I'm not necessarily suggesting hypnosis, but I will suggest that ecstatic experiences have something in common with hypnotic trances. Really, they are simply altered states of consciousness in which we can expand our minds beyond ourselves. (And we never really even do that, because we can't really know anyone else's experiences.)

Nothing I'll suggest in this chapter is in any way supernatural. It may help to think of ecstatic experiences as akin to meditation. In a sense, all we're really doing is meditating on goodness. We'll just use techniques, like drumming, dancing, or chanting to get us into that meditative state. The goal is to silence our thoughts and feelings to allow our truest essence to take center stage in the drama of our mind. From there, we'll allow that deep essence to meditate on what's best for all of us.

Ecstatic Methods

I once attended a lecture on Queen Elizabeth I's cryptographer, John Dee. Dee thought that he could literally gain clairvoyance into Spanish military plans (a sort of Renaissance occult version of James Bond). To do so, he performed seances to talk to angels. He believed that the angels spoke to him and that they gave him number squares, which he concluded were actually a secret code. By decoding them, he invented (or discovered) the language of angels: Enochian. Of course, he didn't think he invented it, but rather received it. The lecturer quipped that, if Dee had been a dancer, the angels would have given him dance steps. Since he was a cryptographer, they gave him a secret code.

Number squares won't work for most of us. Choosing an ecstatic method is a personal choice. If you're a dancer, ecstatic dancing is the obvious choice. If you're a musician, trancey music is likely to be what you'll want. If you know a hypnotherapist or are skilled in self-hypnosis, that may be for you.

What we want is anything that turns off your logical mind, makes you feel transported, and gets you out of your gourd. The techniques for this are different from those for entertainment or even for art. Your religious or spiritual tradition may already have what you need. If this includes chanting, drumming, rattling, singing bowl ringing, or ecstatic dancing, you may already be set.

Listening to trancey music will be quite different from going to a concert. This is distinct from the popular music advertised as "trance music." I have nothing against trance music, but what I'm talking about is anything which that will get you into the ecstatic state we want. I personally find that "trance music" is too discordant for my taste, but you may have different tastes than me.

---

and non-Christian, particularly pagan, religions.

Monotonous percussion, like drumming or rattling, works well. If you go the music route, you may want to get yourself a drum, tambourine, or a pair of rattles. There is also plenty of this on YouTube. A search for *shamanic drumming* or *shamanic rattling* will likely find what you want.[5] The monotony of it puts you in a trance, so you'll want something that won't change much and will go on for quite some time, at least fifteen minutes. I personally like didgeridoo music quite well. Buddhist bells, such as singing bowls can work well too.

I personally like chanting, because I can write my own chants or mantras, which I can repeat over and over. If you want to listen to something while you chant, you could go Eastern with something like Buddhist chanting, or Western with Gregorian chanting. I've found that chanting combines nicely with nature sounds, provided the sounds are also essentially monotonous. Waterfall sounds, ocean waves, river, and rain sounds all work well for this. I'll put them on as background to enhance the trancey-ness of my chanting. I'll also sometimes ring a bell while chanting, which works nicely. But all these are totally optional.

For dance, you'll want to do repetitive movements. I even know one woman who feels closer to Goddess when she belly dances. A lot of belly dance tracks are about five minutes, however, which is not typically long enough. Your music should last at least fifteen minutes to really work well.

Remember that you want to "trance out" and go into the moment. You'll probably want a dance that you can do without thinking too much about it. If it has specific steps, you should have them down. You could also just dance extemporaneously. If you do, I think you'll still want music that is fairly repetitive and trancey.

I personally find music with lyrics I can understand to be distracting for this. I start tuning into what the words are saying, and that distracts me from my goal of trancing out. Something like Gregorian chanting is a bit different, because I don't know what they're saying.

The exception is some sort of holy chant or mantra that more or less fits in with what I'm doing and can easily be pushed to the background in my mind. If Buddhist monks are chanting *om gate gate paragate parasamgate bodhi svaha* over and over again, or Catholic monastics chant *ave Maria*, that will be just fine, even good, because it will add some symbolism.[6]

You can also combine several techniques. Drumming and chant-

---

[5] I don't mean to imply that I think videos with these titles represent authentic shamanism. I've just found that these search terms often find the sorts of trance music I'm after. Whether or not the people who made them should have used the label "shamanic" is another matter.

[6] The Buddhist chant is the Prajnaparamita Mantra. It's pronounced *ome gah-tay gah-tay para-gah-tay para-sam-gah-tay bo-dee sva-ha*. It means something like *Gone! Gone! Gone beyond! Gone utterly beyond! Enlightenment! All hail!*

ing, mantras and singing bowls, music and dance all seem to go well together. As long as you can do each of the forms together and it's not too chaotic to do so, it should work just fine. Experiment! This is your spiritual art project.

I would warn, however, that it's often hard to dance and do anything else. Dancing does not combine well with chanting or singing, for example, if you're the one doing both. However, it *does work* to listen to recorded music, chanting, drumming, and the like while you do your part. I sometimes like to listen to drumming, didgeridoo, or singing bowls in the background while I chant.

The ecstasy can sometimes take some time to start. At first, as we drum, rattle, chant, or dance, we may think a lot about the rhythm, the words, or the steps. The key is to let your mind go and become one with it. Allow your mind to alter. Let yourself be taken up by it.

This is why it's so important that your ecstatic experience occur within a ritual with symbolism that you're in control of. Whatever you were focusing on before will still be with you as you shift into a trancey state of mind. If it's just a party, you'll probably just have fun. If it's a concert, you'll connect with the music. However, that's not likely what we want.

We want all our symbolism and our focus on goodness to fill us completely as our souls begin to soar. Once our state of mind alters, we're on autopilot, as it were. However, if we have all our symbolism and ritual setup right, we'll automatically fly to that secret city of the Monad. We will have already symbolized, to our mind, where we want to go, so our flight will know where to take us.

Remember in the last chapter how there was this main portion in the middle of the ritual that I said I'd explain later? Your ecstatic experience goes there. I didn't unpack that before, because I felt you had enough to focus on with learning ritual design. So I said you could just stick a chant in. You can, but better yet, fill that section in with a full-fledged ecstatic experience (and a chant may well be your tool of choice for that). That makes the ritual complete.

To transcend to the Monad, you'll want to get out your symbolism kit and a ritual you've designed, or else use the symbols and practices of your own religion. Perform your ritual up until you get to the main part. Perform the ecstatic part and trance out for as long as you feel you need to. Your soul will know when to return.[7]

Let your mind go until you get to the perspective that all is one. Because that includes your consciousness, this can feel a little bit like your mind going blank. Your thoughts, feelings, and perceptions are all part of that oneness. When we in the West talk about our minds

---

[7] I don't mean soul in the literal sense of something that survives death, necessarily. A soul, as I mean it, could just be the essence of who you are or some deep part of your consciousness.

going blank, we often use it as a negative, as if the mind is being erased, but I mean something positive. The mind is still there, it's just experiencing oneness. We are not separate from our minds, so the mind—the self—is clear, like a calm lake with no ripples.

This is the Monad. Once there, you'll glimpse the Good. Meditate on it. Take as much time as you need here. Breathe! Experience!

When you're ready to return, slowly start to wind down your ecstatic experience. Slow down the drums, dance, chant, or what have you. Allow your consciousness to come back to normal.

Remember the twenty-four hour rule. Because your thoughts and feelings were part of the oneness, and your mind has cleared, it may take some time for new thoughts and feelings about your experience to form. Wait twenty-four hours, and then I suggest writing down any epiphanies you have in a journal or notebook.

One more note before I move on to guidelines for effective ecstatic experiences. When I talk about transcendence, I'm not claiming that the transcendent is superior to mundane, material reality. I believe in being ethical at all levels of the Tetractys. Ultimately, it is in the material world where we need to act in accordance with our understanding of the Good. However, we find our vision of goodness in the Monad. Both ends are equally important.

Rules for Ecstatic Experiences

Not all ecstatic experiences are deep. Some may be light and short, while others can be long and profound. Experiencing oneness includes a oneness of time, so time can sometimes seem to stand still. Sometimes we go deeper than we plan to, so it's good to just plan ahead beforehand.

Just as with symbolism and ritual, I'm going to suggest several guidelines to you. Like all my rules, these are never meant to insult or coddle anyone. I know my readers are mature adults, who would probably think of these things on their own. It's just that I'd be remiss if I didn't give you a few basic safety tips.

Vacations and ecstatic experiences are both hard to enjoy if you worry you've left the stove on. So make a checklist of things you need to do before you go, and check things off. If you've already put a check by "make sure the stove is off" and "I have a partner who's ready to get the door if the doorbell rings," then you can relax and let yourself be transported.

Rule 1: Have a Partner Assist You

The farther out of our heads we get, the less practical we become. For deep practice, it can be helpful to have someone with you, who will refrain from joining you in your ecstatic experience, so they can watch out for you.

I don't necessarily mean your life partner. This person could also be a trusted friend in your spiritual community. If the doorbell or phone rings, let them answer it (though you should probably have silenced your phone beforehand anyway). Let them take care of mundane things, so you don't have to. If you have children, tell them you'll be meditating but that your partner will help them. Trying to go mundane will break you out of your ecstatic state.

It's good to just have someone make sure you aren't doing anything stupid that will cause harm to you, your home, or anyone living with you. Accidents happen, and the more tranced out we get, the more accident prone we become.

The best way you can thank your partner is by returning the favor. If they're involved with a similar practice, volunteer to keep them safe in the same way. Otherwise, maybe treat them to lunch sometime. Be sure to thank them, whatever the case.

Of course, not everyone has the luxury of a partner. If that's the case, do the best you can on your own, with what you have. I recommend writing out a list of dos and don'ts for yourself ahead of time. Just that simple act tends to pre-program our minds. I often find that I'll naturally remember to do the dos and avoid the don'ts just because I wrote them down. I know it sounds silly, but if I feel I really need to, I may even tape up reminders around my home. Fortunately most of us will only be in an ecstatic state for about fifteen minutes to an hour (and five minutes is fine, too).

Rule 2: Don't Use Power Tools (and So On)
This is a good rule of thumb for things not to attempt. Any situation in which they say "don't use power tools" probably applies to being in an ecstatic state. Don't do anything that might result in burning your home down, like putting candles on the floor near curtains drawn in front of an open window. Don't communicate with anyone you're angry with. Don't sign legal documents. Don't write anything on social media.

Rule 3: Learn a Few Techniques to Bring You Out
In case of an ecstatic emergency (in which you have trouble coming down), have some techniques on hand to ground you very quickly and get you back into a normal state of consciousness, so you can be practical again. Make sure your partner knows these, too.

Patting your body to bring yourself back to physical reality can be good. Drink plenty of water. I also find it helpful to eat protein. You may want to perform the grounding from the last chapter, in which you visualize yourself as a tree with your roots going deep into the earth. For whatever reason, all these techniques bring people quickly down from the trance state.

If those basics don't work, here are some other ideas I've encountered. For some reason, they seem to work. One is to put salt on your tongue. Something about the flavor kicks you right back into a normal state of consciousness. Some people put salt on the crown of their head. (Maybe we just remember that, if our partner is sprinkling salt on our head, it must be time to come back.)

I also recommend simply taking some time to relax after a ritual. Allow yourself to come down gracefully from the high. Instruct your partner ahead of time to check in with you during this process, bringing you water or whatever else you need. If you're practicing at someone else's home, be sure to tell them ahead of time that you may need fifteen minutes or so afterward to just relax.

Ecstatic experiences are perfectly safe. In time you'll naturally come out of them. The main thing is to make sure you're good to drive, so to speak. If not, relax until you are.

Rule 4: Go Into It with a Clear Head
I mentioned purification in the last chapter, but I'll reiterate it here. One purpose of purification in a ritual is to make sure you enter your ecstatic state in an ordinary state of consciousness. As I've already mentioned, it's much easier to return to ordinary consciousness if that's the state we started in.

Rule 5: Let Go Instead of Forcing It
By far the biggest problem people have with ecstatic experiences is not safety, but rather feeling that it didn't work. The problem is that we often mistake our thoughts and feelings for ourselves. It's hard to feel at one with everything if we hold on to our thoughts and feelings.

The key is to be receptive, rather than active. Try to let go, rather than forcing it. It's not something you do, so much as something that you allow to happen. Listen to the drums, get lost in the dance, be one with the chant. Let your technique fill your beings. Take a leap of faith. Let yourself be carried off by it.

One reason why we take safety precautions is to allow ourselves to feel safe letting go. If you know you won't be disturbed and your partner is there to make sure you don't burn the house down, you're good. Even if you don't have a partner, if you've made the proper preparations, I think you'll be fine.

Rule 6: Batten Down the Hatches
Before you start your ritual, what I recommend is lock and latch the front door. If you have a back door, do the same. If you have housemates and you don't want to be disturbed, it may not be overkill to lock the door to the room where you'll be performing the ritual, as

well. Doing all this will just give you that extra assurance that you'll remain safe and undisturbed throughout the ritual.

Rule 7: Be Responsible
This isn't so much another rule as it is a reiteration of all the other rules. The main point is to take this work seriously and be a responsible adult who uses common sense.

Sample Chants
Here are some chants you can use. Some of these are straightforward, while others use a kind of poetry that's not so much logical as trance-inducing. Some are easy to use, right out of the gate, while others require more practice but are also potentially richer and more trancey.

I recommend trying a chant that you think will be just the right amount of challenge to put you into a flow state. If it's so easy that you can think about other things while you're chanting, it's probably too easy. If it's so hard that you stumble over the words, even after a little practice, it's too complex.

Choose what works for you. Each chant takes up one line.
- All are one. One is all.[8]
- I am we. We are one. We are one and I am we.
- I am we. We are one. One are we and we am I.
- I am all are one.
- I am we are all are one.
- I am all are one are all am I.
- North south east west. I am they. We are one.[9]
- North south east west. We are all. All are one.[10]
- Water earth fire air. I am they. We are one.[11]
- Water earth fire air. We are all. All are one.
- North south east west. Above below center. All are one.
- We are above. We are below. We are all the center.
- I am they and they are we and we are all the center.
- I rise above and I am they and they are we and we are one.

---

8 This one, and the next, are extremely simple and to the point.
9 I like this one, because it follows the Tetractys. First there are four words for the Tetrad marking the compass points: *north south east west*. Then there are three words for the Triad: *I am they*. Then two for the Dyad: *we are*. One for the Monad: *one*.
10 This one's very similar in that regard. However, the first one is better for one person alone, whereas this one is conducive to a group.
11 These next two are exactly the same as the last two, except I've replaced the four directions with the four elements, in case some people relate to that better.

Having an Ecstatic Experience

It's time. You're ready. All the symbolism and ritual you did before has led up to this. I'd like you to try a short ecstatic experience.

It could just be fifteen minutes for your first one. Pick a technique. Do you like drumming? Dancing? Chanting? Singing? Singing bowls? Gregorian chant? Mantras? With experience, you may even experiment, in your own good time, with combining some of these, but it takes trial and error to find out which techniques can work together and which ones clash. If you don't have a technique in mind, you might want to pick one of the chants I've presented above.

Of course, as I've said, all this will be better when in the context of ritual and symbolism. This first time through is just to get some practice. In the next chapter, I'll present a full-blown ritual that has all the pieces: mythic symbolism, ritual, and ecstatic experience. For now, all I'll ask is to do the best you can with this piece. The chants I wrote all have symbolism in them, so I think you'll find any of them will work pretty well.

I'll advise that you follow the rules above. Allow yourself to really let go. Allow your symbolism to take you to the Good (or as close to It as you can without all the mythic and ritual around it).

Don't worry if you don't go into a trance the first time. It's better if it's a trance, but it doesn't need to be. In actuality, it all probably worked much better than you think. Just doing a ritual in which you chant poetry about the oneness is good, in and of itself. Practice makes perfect. You can do it!

The goal is really just to have a direct experience of goodness. If you get beyond yourself, as it were, and feel unified with all humanity, all life, or the cosmos, that's really it. I believe that we get our concepts of goodness from experiences like this. As we say in Wicca, blessed be!

8

The Journey up the Tetractys

I sit in the center of my temple room with a bell in front of me. Incense still burns on the altar. I still get a whiff of brine from the salt water I've sprinkled around. I focus on a drawing I've made of people holding hands in a circle at the crossroads. In their center is Mother Earth. This symbolizes all humanity as one.

I ring the bell and begin to chant, "I am we! We are one! We are one, and I am we!" I continue chanting this, accenting it with the bell periodically, until the meaning of the words fades and I'm left with the music of their poetry. My mind is caught up in those sounds. It goes blank, but all my symbolism guides it as it transcends my selfhood to something greater.

A couple days later, I journal about my experience. Now that I've had a vision of unity, how I ought to treat my fellow people seems so much clearer.

Let's put the last three chapters together into one practice. So far, I've invited you to create your symbol kit, to experiment with ritual, and to experiment with ecstatic experience. In this chapter I'm going to invite you to work all three together and actually undertake the full journey that leads to the Monad.

This is the big one! I'm going to suggest that you set aside at least half a day for this and maybe the day after to decompress. This will be a ritual with an ecstatic experience at the heart of it, which I'll call your first journey. The journey itself may only take about an hour or two to perform, but you'll want time to prepare beforehand and time to absorb it after you're done. If you have the weekend off, a Saturday would be ideal, because you can process it Sunday morning without having to be distracted by work. You may well go on other journeys, and I hope you do.

It might not take all day, but I'm suggesting that you take the whole day as a spiritual retreat anyway. Unplug from TV, videos, partying, and all the normal things you do to occupy your mind. It's not that there's anything wrong with those things; it's that we're trying to gain perspective.

If you can't take a whole day off, that's fine, too. Just a few hours' retreat may be right for you.

The more you practice the Religion of Good, the less time you'll need to set aside, because the less your brain will need to process it. As I've said in previous chapters, I highly recommend making sure you won't be disturbed.

I'm going to give you a full script that you can use. I'll follow all my rules. I won't give you anything explicitly Wiccan, since that would be counterproductive to all but my own community. Instead, I'll give you something more generic that I believe people from most religions or spiritualities will find useful. Perforce, this will closely resemble a Wiccan ritual, because that's what I know best. I feel it would be better for me to give you a ritual style I know very well than one I don't. However, it won't actually be Wicca in terms of religious content.

This script is one approach. It focuses on coming to an understanding of all sentient beings as one. However, as I've said, you could also use the Religion of Good to contemplate specific kinds of good, like liberty or love, or to balance various virtues like mercy and severity. All the knowledge you need is in the last three chapters.

You could take a different path to goodness, too. Earlier in this book, I described finding a balance between self-discipline and compassion, with love in the middle. You could even organize a practice around an epic, such as throwing an evil ring into a volcano, navigating a labyrinth, or descending into the underworld to give guidance to your inner demons. I'm just keeping things simple so you can experience one example of a full journey. In "Appendix I: Recipes for Goodness", I'll include additional journeys you can experiment with.

I'd invite you to treat this as a recipe in a sort of spiritual cookbook that we're working on together. Try it! See what you think. Feel free to modify it to suit your own religious or spiritual needs, just as you might add cinnamon or remove marjoram from a recipe. I encourage you to make your own recipes. The most important thing is that I'd like you to actually do the full practice I give you here. Since it is ultimately ineffable, the only way to understand it is to do it. Practice makes perfect.

Here's the format of the journey. We'll start out with symbols of the material world, such as salt, water, fire, incense smoke, and the four compass directions. From there, we'll honor and celebrate our symbol of unity, taking us up the Tetractys. First to the Triad, because we're using symbolism, then to the Dyad, because we've symbolized the unity of all people. Then we'll chant to get the final way up to the Monad. Finally, we'll reverse the journey, thanking Mother Earth, and then concluding with final salutes to the compass points and grounding ourselves back in the Tetrad.

What You'll Need
1. A blank piece of paper to draw on
2. Colored markers, crayons, or colored pencils to draw with
3. Salt (table salt is fine)
4. A salt box (or any container to put the salt in)
5. A bowl of water (tap water is fine)
6. An incense censer
7. Incense in the censer
8. Matches
9. A surface to use as an altar, such as a table
10. OPTIONAL: A bell (a Buddhist bowl bell would be ideal, but any will work)
11. OPTIONAL: A compass (if you don't know which way north is)
12. OPTIONAL: Some colorful cloth to use as an altar cloth

Mythic Symbolism

To keep things simple, I'm going to suggest that we focus on symbolizing all of humanity as one. Draw a picture of a circle of people holding hands with the world in the center. If your spiritual tradition uses angels, draw little angels helping everyone hold hands. You could also substitute spirits or Buddhas for this. Your art doesn't have to be worthy of the Louvre. There's no shame in stick figures.

In fact, while you could print out an image online or even use statuary for this, I'm going to suggest that you draw this yourself. By doing so, you'll put your own energy into it, so to speak. I was taught that the effort of creating a picture like this adds power to the practice you use it for. What I mean by this is that, in drawing this, your mind will already start to engage with the mythic symbolism. It's actually better to do it yourself in a humble, mediocre way than to have someone else create high art for you. (Of course, if you're a visual artist, you can have your cake and eat it, too.)

My second suggestion is that we use Mother Earth as our symbol of all humanity coming together on this planet. Mother Earth is no more a Goddess than Lady Liberty. She's the personification of an idea: everyone on our planet as one. It's true that in Wicca we revere an earth Goddess, but there's a difference between the religious reverence for an intelligent deity and a symbol.

I think that people of all religions can relate to our planet itself as a symbol of unity. If you're still concerned, perhaps you could say "Angel Earth", in reference to the guardian angel of our planet. However you conceive of her (or him or it), draw Mother Earth in the center of the ring of people, to represent this unity.

Finally, I'm going to suggest that we need a connecting symbol between the ring of people and Mother Earth. The crossroads is a powerful mythic symbol in many cultures. The crossroads join countries and societies. It is the intersection of ideas. It's where we stand when we make major decisions. I'm suggesting that you draw lines from each person in the ring to Mother Earth to represent the great Crossroads of Humanity, through which we communicate, travel to meet each other, and interact.

Putting it all together, your picture should show a ring of people. Inside of that ring should be the Crossroads of Humanity. Standing there should be Mother Earth. I'll leave it as an art project for you exactly how to draw all this.

Setup

Setup for the ritual in the space you've set aside for it. Cover the surface you'll use with your altar cloth. This can be any colorful piece of cloth big enough to cover your surface. You can also simply cover a piece of floor or an area of a desk. If you don't have a cloth, you can omit the altar cloth. This surface is now your altar for the duration of the practice.

I don't recommend trying this on a bed, but if that's all you have, you'll probably want a solid surface like a board on it to keep the water bowl from spilling. You'll also want to take all appropriate fire safety measures.

Place your salt box, water bowl, censer, incense, matches, and picture on the altar. Make sure your incense is in the censer and ready to be lit. Do a final check to make sure you have everything. It would be a shame to have to, say, run off to find the matches. You'll also want to get yourself a compass (or a compass app for your device). Be sure you know, roughly, which directions are north, south, east, and west. I usually just approximate so that either each wall or each corner of the room I'm working in corresponds to one of the cardinal directions.

As with all the practices in this book, this is duplicated in Appendix I and laid out in a format that is more conducive to actually performing it, whereas I've put more of the whys and wherefores here.

Grounding

Sit or stand comfortably. Close your eyes. Visualize yourself as a tree. See your roots going deep into the earth. They are going into the Tetrad: the material world. Reach your hands above your head, spreading your fingers. Reach these, your "branches," up to the sky, up to the Monad and the light of the Good.

Say: **I am here. I am here. I am here.**

Purification

Touch the water bowl and say, **The waters of intuition.** Take a pinch of salt in your hand from the salt box and say, **The salt of the earth.** Mix the salt into the water in the bowl. Sprinkle yourself with just a few drops of salt water.

Now, go counterclockwise around your space, sprinkling just a little salt water. As you do so, chant the following over and over until you've circled all the way around back to your altar:

By Water and Earth,
Full once around,
In the name of the All
I hallow this ground.
Before It must
All evil flee.
This is my will:
So mote it be.[1]

When you've come back around to your altar, set the water bowl back down.

Blessing

Touch the censer lightly so as not to dislodge the incense. Say, **The air of clarity.** With the incense in the censer, light the incense with the matches and say, **The fire of will.** Wave the incense smoke over yourself and proceed to move around the area clockwise, waving the incense over everything. As you do so, chant the following over and over again:

By Fire and Air,
Full once around,
In the name of the One
I hallow this ground.
Before It must
All evil flee.
This is my will:
So mote it be.

Creating Sacred Space and Time

Ring the bell. Walk around the area clockwise, ring it. As you do, chant the following:

---

[1] This and the next chant are both paraphrased from a song by Valerie Voigt, which is used in the Waxing Moon tradition of Wicca. Her song was inspired by a spoken chant by Sally Eaton. It is used with permission.

Circle, circle, round about,
With One and All throughout and about!

Recreating the Cosmos

Face east.
Say: **Angels of the rising sun, brighten my soul to know the Good**
Face south.
Say: **Angels of the warm south, stoke my will to see the Good**
Face west.
Say: **Angels of the setting sun, help me dare to meet the Good**
Face north.
Say: **Angels of the cold north, temper me to receive the Good**[2]

Calling the Characters

Face your picture on the altar. Focus on the ring of humans around the Crossroads of Humanity, at the center of which stands Mother Earth. Let's salute this image by chanting the following chant three times through.

Mother Earth Blue and Green,
Global Girth and Crossroad Queen.

Honor the whole picture with a bow. Even though Mother Earth is just a symbol, the concept of all of us united is real and worthy of honor.

The Chant of Oneness

Next, I'll give you a chant you can use for the ecstatic portion for the ritual (which follows).

Begin this chant slowly. At first, there's the mechanical act of reciting it accurately. That involves remembering the words and getting the cadence down. It's a simple enough chant, so it shouldn't be hard to get the words down, but you will want to get them right so that you'll go into a flow state. It can take time to get into the groove. After a while, though, it takes less and less focus to make sure we have the words right. We can relax and go on autopilot, allowing the words to flow.

You could easily accompany the chant with your bell or another

---

[2] The traditional Wiccan order for saluting the directions comes from the apparent movement of the sun in the Northern Hemisphere: rising in the east, slightly south of the equator at noon, setting in the west, and slightly north of the equator at midnight. Some Wiccans in the Southern Hemisphere reverse this order to reflect the apparent counterclockwise movement of the sun in that part of the world: north, west, south, east. You can also reverse some of the attributions, such as exchanging *cold* and *warm* for north and south, and putting *stoke my will* in the warm north and *temper my soul* in the cold south.

percussion instrument. You could dance while chanting it (though many people have trouble doing those two things at the same time). I like to put on appropriate music, like Tibetan singing bowls or didgeridoo music. Maybe for you, Gregorian chant works. The main thing is for it to harmonize. When in doubt, I use ocean wave sounds. The sea goes with everything! All these things are good if they augment the chant, but bad if they distract from it. Here's the chant.

I am we.
We are one.
We are one
And I am we.[3]

Keep chanting until you go into a trance. I don't mean a hypnotized state like in the movies, but a state of mind in which you let go of conscious thoughts and feelings and just chant. The meaning of the words may even fade into the background, and their sounds may become like music. For me, this chant becomes almost like a buzz or thrum, like a bullroarer.

At this point, let your mind go. Everything prior to this moment has been a symbolic ritual meant to program your inner autopilot. Your mind knows where to go, and it is on course to the Good. Keep chanting.

Keep up this altered state for some time: as long as you feel you should. Relax and stay there until you're ready to conclude. Ironically, although I keep using a journey metaphor, this state is—for now—exactly where you want to be in your mind. You'll know when to stop.

I'll talk later about what happened. For now, I'll ask you to have faith that this very act is developing your personal relationship with goodness. All will be explained next chapter.

Thanking the Characters
Once you're ready to continue, bow to the picture on the altar and say the following:

Mother Earth!
Thank you for your blessing.
You are with us always.

Releasing the Cosmos
Face north.

---

[3] This chant is very simple and to the point. If you'd like something a little more advanced and trancey, you could reverse the words of the last two lines so that the chant goes like this: *I am we. We are one. One are we and we am I.*

Say: **Angels of the cold north, thank you for your blessing**
Face west.
Say: **Angels of the setting sun, thank you for your blessing**
Face south.
Say: **Angels of the warm south, thank you for your blessing**
Face east.
Say: **Angels of the rising sun, thank you for your blessing**[4]

Decommissioning Sacred Space and Time

Lift the bell and ring it. Walk around your space counterclockwise ringing it. As you do, chant the following:

> *Work done!*
> *Web spun!*
> *Circle end*
> *Where 'twas begun.*[5]

Grounding Afterward

Repeat the tree meditation above. Feel rooted in the earth and the material world once more. Visualize your roots going deep down into the earth and drawing nutrients up from Mother Earth. Your journey is complete, but it hasn't finished impacting you.

Next, I suggest that you do something fun and relaxing (though I wouldn't jump too quickly into anything social, just because it may be a bit much after such a deep experience). Remember the twenty-four hour rule. Avoid talking about what you did with others or even writing or thinking too much about it. You may want to jot down a few short notes in a journal while ideas are fresh, but at this point keep it sketchy, just some cues to remind yourself of your thoughts. There's a happy medium between record keeping and overthinking, so stay on the record keeping side of this.

After that, try to shift your mind away from all the work you've been doing. Let it percolate in the background, while you get on with life. A feast would be ideal. Having wonderful food, while allowing your mind to drift is great. A ritual bath or a dip in the hot tub, if you have one, can work well, too. Maybe hike in the woods. Think both fun and sacred. I wouldn't do anything too taxing. You've worked hard! Now is a time to take a well-earned rest. When you're ready, move on to the next chapter, in which I will explain what just happened and why that's everything.

After you've practiced this enough times, you can probably be less oriented toward a one-person spiritual retreat in your home. Putting that together can be a lot of work. The first time through, it's worth it.

---

4 Again, folks down under should feel free to change *cold north* and *warm south*.
5 This is how we "open circle" in the Waxing Moon tradition of Wicca.

As you get more familiar with the practice, you'll probably be able to set aside less and less time. Eventually, following up with mundane forms of entertainment, like movies, will probably be fine and feel natural. I just want you to really set time aside the first time through, so that you allow space in your life for it to be powerful.

Practice Makes Perfect

What if this practice didn't go as expected? That is, what if your mind didn't go blank in the chant? Maybe you don't feel you got much out of it.

They say practice makes perfect. Keep trying! Before assuming it didn't work, though, I'd like to share an episode of the 1990s TV show *Northern Exposure* with you. Joel Fleischman, the doctor of the fictional town of Cecily, Alaska, is taken on a vision quest by Northwest native Ed Chigliak. Looking up at the moon, in the middle of the Alaskan wilderness, Joel doesn't think he had a vision, but Ed says, *Well, maybe you did.*

Well, maybe you did. But you may not know it until you've waited a day or so (another reason for the twenty-four hour rule).

And even if you didn't, nothing's perfect and we'll never be perfect. Perfection is never achievable, but it's ever approachable. The more you practice, the better you'll get.

If you really think it didn't work, even after a few days have passed, I'd encourage you to start by repeating the practice in this chapter (the whole ritual with the trance-out chant in the middle). If you'd like to change it, I think you know by now what my answer is: By all means, please do.

If you've given it a few good tries, though, and you just don't like it, that's fine with me. I'm inviting you to climb the Tetractys any which way you can. If choir music or a good old mass does that for you better than my ritual, by all means, go to church. If meditation accomplishes the same goal, by all means meditate. If you create a ritual that works better for you, that's wonderful. There are many techniques to achieve a direct experience of the Good. Use whatever works for you, but I hope you will use it.

Take the Journey

Your homework for this chapter is to take the journey I've described above. As mentioned above, for your convenience I've put this ritual under "Ritual of Oneness" in Appendix I, "Recipes for Goodness".

Please wait twenty-four hours before reading the next chapter, so that you've given your journey time to percolate.

9

The Jewel to Take Home

I sit in front of my word processor, musing about what I think good is. I remember the ideas that came to me from my last journey. I've opened a living file that I keep editing. It contains the statement of my personal ethics. I know it's fallible, because I'm fallible.

I won't tell you what it says (though I did put one set of thoughts in Appendix IV, "The Virtues of a Free Society"). After all, I'm not writing this book to preach ethics at you, but rather to offer some thoughts on how you might refine your own ethics through spirituality. Every time I complete a journey, I reread this statement and revise it with ideas from my latest vision of the Good.

I'm less agitated and more content than I used to be, because I have more ethical clarity. But it's not just that. As I clarify my own ethical uncertainty through the Religion of Good practice, I find I have more respect for other value systems. Admitting my lack of clarity before the journey, gaining more clarity after, and finally seeing that I'll never have perfect knowledge of ethics reminds me that I'm just another human being trying to do the right thing. It's somehow easier to engage with others when I'm clearer on my ethics, but also when I realize that they may have different but equally authentic values from my own.

Welcome back from the Monad. You visited the Monad when your mind went blank during the chant while performing the practice in the last chapter. Now you've returned.

At least twenty-four hours have passed since the ritual, so you should welcome any and all thoughts about goodness. Go ahead and talk to others about it. Write down your experience and the thoughts that come to you.

You may ask at this point, *When did I make contact with the Good?* It may seem like all you did was a ritual with a lot of chanting in the middle. You made contact when your mind went blank. Since the

Good is at the Monad, where all is one, and the Good is ineffable and mysterious, thoughts and feelings would have taken you back down the Tetractys. You needed to have that pure moment of ineffable oneness to have your direct experience of goodness.

In the last twenty-four hours, you've been slowly returning to the Tetrad. This process is almost effortless, because understanding reality in material terms is our normal state of mind. It's like floating on a raft down a calm river. All you need to do is allow yourself to drift. Because thoughts can't happen in the Monad, we don't unpack our experience until this point of return.

Remember the Alan Watts quote from earlier in this book? *Reality is* — [rings bell] — *and we won't give it a name*. Your pure, non-thinking, direct experience needed to be refined into something more comprehensible than that bell ringing, in order for you to able to have thoughts about it.

Remember several chapters back when I encouraged you to take stock of the material world, because that's the world you'd come back to? Now you understand why. Goodness cannot be found in the material world, but we perform good deeds *in* the material world. We contemplate our journey in the material world. We interact with others in the material world. It's vital to have a stable material world to return to, *so that* you can best contemplate your vision in the Monad and begin to manifest it.

Write down all the ideas about goodness that come to you. You may find that you're starting to see things differently. Some sense of goodness is coming through. Maybe it's simply that you're feeling more loving toward everyone. If that's it, that's wonderful! These thoughts are your thoughts. As I've been saying throughout this book, none of us knows the truth, but I believe that we all have a conscience. Someone else going on this journey may have different thoughts. They may have different assumptions, different cultural values, different metaphysics, different views on teleology, or just a different worldview in general from your own. That's okay. It's also okay that some people won't go on this journey. Their thoughts about ethics may also be valid. There are other approaches to dealing with the ethics crisis. For some, Reason is a valid spiritual path. For others, their religion guides them.

In the Pagan community (the larger community of adherents of Pagan religions, of which Wicca is only one part), we talk about UPG: Unverified Personal Gnosis. If someone feels that some deity has "spoken" to them, we neither affirm nor deny it, but simply say, *That's your UPG*. If we like what they report, we'll say, *That's good UPG*. It's common for us to understand no one as a prophet, but everyone as having the ability to receive messages from the Divine.

Maybe God tells one person one thing and another person another, based on what each person needs to hear at that time in their life. Or maybe you believe that God never speaks directly to ordinary people. That's all fine.

And, anyway, in this book, we're not speaking literally. I'm not writing about Good as Divine, because for our purposes it doesn't matter whether it is or not. I do believe it's real and that, like God, it's ineffable and mysterious.

So none of this discussion of different worldviews is to say that goodness itself is relative. I think it's more likely that goodness is real, but none of us ever sees it clearly. I'm also aware of how our worldviews can tint the lenses through which we see that reality.

You probably got something valid from the Good, but it doesn't mean it's the only valid thing someone can get, or that your UPG won't conflict with someone else's (or even your own!). Sometimes paradox can even be a good thing, as long as we take it as an opportunity to slow down and maybe meditate to see if we can find some way through. I find that balancing various seemingly conflicting ideas can help. Work hard to feed your family, but money isn't everything, for example.

It can also help to understand that categories are bell curves, not boxes. Sometimes one ethic is in the middle of a bell curve, while others are at the periphery, like you can say anything you want (middle), but don't yell *Fire!* in a crowded theater (periphery).

Speaking of which, just because you came to see something as right, doesn't mean it is. Society needs to protect people from harm, which is why we have laws against things like murder and theft. There's an old joke: What's the difference between preachers and con artists? Preacher believe their own con. Well, not all preachers, of course, just the bad ones.

The point is to try to avoid conning yourself. If you decided that it would be good to, say, punch someone you hate in the nose or something else that seems pretty obviously bad to most of us, you're very likely conning yourself. The goal is to have insights and epiphanies about goodness, rather than to replace common sense.

Remember what I said in Chapter 1: Check intuition with reason and reason with intuition. *The Religion of Good is never an excuse for murder or any other kind of violence or harm.* It *is* about gaining ethical insight through spiritual practice, and I am suggesting that that's the way out of the ethics crisis.

For the remainder of this chapter, I'm going to trust that you've taken a good enough look in the mirror. Only you know if you haven't.

Your direct experience of the Good is *typically* good UPG, for you. What you got was probably what you need at this time. I firmly believe that it is wrong for any of us to browbeat another into accepting our vision of goodness. That starts holy wars. Instead, I hope that we can come together as peers and equals within a free society and compare our goodness poetry, as it were.

Speaking of which, now would be an excellent time for you to write real poetry about your experience. Or paint it, sculpt it, make music about it. We cannot express the ineffable through prose. We can, however, express it through the arts. If you have a creative outlet, now is an excellent time to use it to express your vision. If you don't, now is a great time to try your hand at creativity. Share your vision as art and admire the art of others. What you got from your ineffable encounter is the jewel to take home.

I got this idea from Joseph Campbell's concept of the hero's journey, which he explains in his book *The Hero with a Thousand Faces*. At the end of the epic, the hero has some treasure to take home to society. You can now take your insights to guide your own ethical intuition. You can also share them with others, as long as you do so in the peer-to-peer way I'm suggesting.

Our society, and indeed everyone on our planet, may benefit from the myriad ethical insights of all eight billion of us. We are all diamonds in the rough in a heap of uncut stones. As you more clearly refine your own ethics, you may want to share your thoughts with others, with polite civility. Others may benefit from your insights, and you from theirs.

I'll suggest that the key is to open a dialog with your fellow people, rather than preach on a street corner. I'd be prepared for the fact that many people will disagree with you. Let me further suggest that our goal would be to share rather than to argue. Most of us have our own ethical convictions. Preaching against them will only create social discord. Presenting your ideas as food for thought will allow them to pick and choose from the ethical potluck of their peers, your ethics included.

Moreover, a polite but lively discussion of ethics may have value for everyone, you included. By entering the public forum with our ethical insights, we have an opportunity to encounter different ethics than our own. It will be useful to us for others to challenge our ethical convictions and useful to them for us to challenge theirs—so long as we're all honest and polite about what we really think (and yes, I believe that we can and should be both polite and honest).

Alternatively, some of us are more introverted or contemplative. We may want to sit with our ideas, try them out, and just be good people. Others may learn from your example (and you from theirs).

I think the key to leading by example is that less is more. Getting our egos out of the way, trying to avoid posing, just living, and allowing people to find inspiration in us is what I think that really means. And ... if you're hoping others will be inspired by your example, it's only fair turnabout to see if their example inspires you, too.

For some it might not be a matter of dialoguing at all. Just clarifying our ethics, constantly improving ourselves, and being the best people we know how to be is the work of a lifetime, and there are few things more worthwhile than that.

This process of iterative journeying may lead you to ask further questions about ethics. When this happens, it may be time to take another journey. Prepare your mythic symbol set. Get ready for your ritual. Choose a chant, or some other means of having an ecstatic experience. Remember that you can use your own religion to do all this, too, if that works for you. Schedule some time for this journey. Then perform your ritual, become ecstatic, transcend yourself, get a handle on the Good, return, meditate on what you experienced, and then reengage with society with this new understanding.

We thus refine our souls, through a lifetime of practice.[1] In the next and final chapter, I'll explain why I think the Religion of Good is the solution to the ethics crisis, and further develop my vision for group practice.

Write a Personal Ethical Statement

I'd like you to write out a statement of your personal ethics. It doesn't have to be a good one. A mediocre one stands head and shoulders above none at all. This is for you and only you (unless you choose to share it). You can refine this and change this as much as you need to. It's just your working theory about how to be a good person. Allow the ideas that came to you after your journey to influence this. Save this in an important place that you won't forget. As you go through more journeys, this will become a living document that you can keep refining.

---

[1] I don't necessarily mean a literal soul, like the one that some believe goes to Heaven after we die. I mean the essence that makes each of us unique and alive.

10
The Good Life

It's my hope that, if enough of us practice the Religion of Good, we'll slowly start to cause the murky waters of our collective goodness to clear. Maybe the point isn't to agree so much as to synergize our ethical ideas and soften the conflicts that inevitably arise. After many iterations of the journey, our most essential selves (our souls, if you will) gain a better and clearer intuition of goodness, just like that murky water.

As you continue to practice, I think you'll find that this practice gets easier and easier. You may need to set aside less and less time. You may find that the practice shortens, but that you can do it more frequently. Eventually you may refine your ritual techniques to the point where you can even make this a daily practice. In fact, that's how I use it most of the time (though I may still take the occasional stay-at-home retreat when I really need it).

I've found that regular practice causes me to spiral up, as it were, and I hope you find that too. As I spiral up, I find that I see the big picture much better and have an easier time with both the intuition and reasoning about ethics in general, and this informs specific ethical questions. As my love for other sentient beings grows, my ethical intuition grows with it, and vice versa.

I hope that you'll find, as I have, a certain sort of contentment in this. It's hard to be good if you're never sure what good is. It's much easier when you've contemplated it through transcendent experiences. I think that we're happier people when we dance with the Good in this way. Keep goodness on your dance card!

Let's reexamine the strategies for ignoring the ethics crisis that I described at the beginning of this book. Does the Religion of Good respond to each of them?

First, there's Creationism, which denies evolution. The Religion of Good does not require evolution or God. Instead, it invites us to transcend our ordinary perspective on the material world (which we may still understand through science) to find the Good. Note, too, that I don't think transcendence is superior to the manifest world, since our most important good acts are in the material world. You can use the Religion of Good equally well whether you agree with the science behind evolution or you believe in Creationism.

Next, I talked about how traditional religion looks to faith for its goodness, but I pointed out that that leads to different ideologies, as each religion relies on its own scripture to inform its morals. I discussed how this can lead to clashes of faith, such as Christian/Muslim or Jewish/Muslim, Muslim/Hindu, Christian/Hindu, Christian/Pagan, and so on. The Religion of Good does not rely on God or on faith in any scripture. Instead, it invites the faithful of many faiths to use their respective scriptures as their mythic symbol set, as well as allowing any of us, even those without a specific faith, to find or make our own symbol set in order to help us all climb the Tetractys. Anybody, religious or non-, can use the Religion of Good equally well.

I talked about how some people understand the amorality of nature to imply that we should be amoral. Many contemporary philosophers, as I understand, doubt this line of thinking according to something they call the *is-ought* logical fallacy. Just because something in nature *is* so, does not imply that we *ought* to act accordingly.

Anyone who's really committed to being amoral won't make use of my practice because they won't think it's important. However, anyone who's fallen into the amorality trap because they don't believe in God and don't find morality in nature *can* use the sort of practice I've prescribed to gain ethical insight, because it will help them transcend the material world to a vision of unity.

I then pointed out that a simplistic type of empathy can be unbalanced or misplaced. People can manipulate us with false emotions. They can also lack sufficient self-discipline to temper their real ones. Empathy is a virtue, but must be balanced against other virtues to be useful, otherwise we might end up coddling weakness instead of caring legitimately.

By helping us transcend ourselves, having a direct experience of the Good, and seeing all as one, we can see more easily where to situate empathy among various virtues, mindful that true compassion and love can illuminate simplistic empathy, by causing us to look more deeply into ethical questions and sometimes calling us to stand up for important causes. We can shine in the light of wisdom to refine empathy as a significant tool in our toolbox and, thus, grow in our craft as good people.

I then questioned discipline. I pointed out that the Nazis were disciplined but totally uncompassionate, for example, and argued first that we specifically want self-discipline in a free society, but that even that does not really answer ethical questions per se. It's just one thing we'd need to implement through our ethics once we've clarified what we think is right.

Again, the Religion of Good helps us shine the light of wisdom in, because it helps us transcend to see the big picture: the unity of all conscious beings. By doing so, we discover what it is we need to cultivate in ourselves in order to be good people and where self-discipline fits into that.

I also inquired about moral relativism. Can we afford to allow every culture and every individual to have a completely separate set of ethics? How would we interact? On the other hand, people need to be able to have their own opinions about ethics. How do we have one ethical system, and allow everyone to have their own opinions? Neither way seems to work. While cultural relativism and personal relativism seem to form a liberal utopia, in fact completely separate and incompatible ethical systems lead toward warring ideologies that threaten to tear apart our free society and the world.

There's a difference between moral relativism on the one hand and a reality about goodness that none of us knows. As I've said throughout the course of this book, I believe that goodness is real but that it's an ineffable mystery. Likewise, there's a difference between moral relativism, which has no concept of a moral reality, and ethical pluralism, in which different cultures have different perspectives on goodness. The idea that many cultures and people have equally good and equally flawed understandings of goodness is very different from the idea that it's purely relative all the way down.

We need some way to synergize our ethics in order to find some common ground in which to act according to each of our ethical systems. The Religion of Good provides a common practice, within our respective systems, without prescribing a specific ethical code. Even if we see different visions of goodness, it is my hope that we can come together around that process. We'll need enough humility to realize that each of our visions is flawed.[1] This is the common ground we need to synergize. More on this in just a bit.

After that, I discussed how ethical intuition *won't* work. You might wonder if I'm contradicting myself. My point, then, was threefold: first, that intuition does not allow us to *know* what's good, because others may have different intuitions; second, that there's no way to resolve clashes between different people with different intuitions; and third, that intuition alone is inadequate, unless it's informed by something else.

The Religion of Good is that something else. The intuitions we're refining with it are informed by our transcendent, ecstatic experiences. If it's true that goodness is real, our transcendent experiences of it provide the missing piece, by informing our ethical intuition, even though these experiences don't help us gain knowledge in a ra-

---

[1] By humility, I simply mean a lack of arrogance. I believe in a type of humility that is informed by self-esteem and good ego. In the end, all I mean by it is the realization that we're all equal.

tional sense. The journey provides us with a common vision of unity, even though we see that vision with the same accuracy that the blind people feel the elephant.

We don't come to know better than anyone else. However, these experiences *do* provide us with a framework for our intuition that helps us get a handle on our own ethics, through some gnosis of an ineffable and mysterious Good. Intuition without our journey lacks that framework.

Part of the Religion of Good practice that I've hoped to express in this book is toleration for other ethical visions. While our common vision of unity may not resolve ethical differences, by practicing humility in our approach to the journey and remembering that it's personal for all of us, we remember to allow others to have their own visions of goodness.

What about the Golden Rule (treat others as *you'd* want to be treated)? Do we follow the Golden Rule even to the point where extroverts force their attention on introverts or introverts don't interact with extroverts? Do we follow the Platinum Rule (treat others the way *they* want to be treated) to the point of giving heroin to heroin addicts?

As I've said, I think the Golden Rule is great, but it's a wisdom teaching, rather than a purely rational solution. The vision we receive from the Religion of Good (or some comparable technique) provides us with the context we're lacking in applying the Golden Rule. We can see that the wisdom of the Golden Rule is for extroverts to treat introverts as if they, the extroverts, were introverted, because we are all one, and ditto for how introverts should treat extroverts.

Except that it's not that simple, because I think the true Golden Rule is ineffable. I think that that mystic, Jesus of Nazareth, taught it, because I think he must have had a great deal of insight into the transcendent and, from there, the Good.[2]

This wisdom also guides us to help heroin addicts get rehabilitated, rather than to help them use, because, although we may enjoy heroin, we'd certainly not enjoy being addicted to it. In other words, the Golden Rule is a call for us to try to think about the effects our actions have on others. The vision of oneness we get from the Religion of Good helps us with that process, because the practice transcends the logic of us versus them and replaces it with a meditation on all of us together. From there, we can apply the wisdom of the Golden Rule from the vantage point of unity.[3]

I pointed out that love can, if poorly managed, paradoxically lead

---

2 I'm being careful here neither to affirm nor to deny his divinity.
3 I personally like a similar concept, sometimes referred to as the Law of the Square, which states things as follows: *Do not do to others as you would hate to have done to you.*

to hatred. Unless we're saints, we can easily become angered when our love is repaid with nastiness. When that happens, we lash out hatefully at those we tried to love. I said that love is a great virtue and a good start, though. True *agape* (love for all people, as opposed to *philos*, love only for friends and family, or *eros*, love for lovers) only really comes into us when we've had a vision of oneness, like the ones that can be had using the Religion of Good. So this kind of love is also ineffable.

The Religion of Good is nothing new. I didn't make it up. I'm just giving a name to the nameless and putting forward my particular technique for realizing goodness. I guarantee you that all saints, sages, and Buddhas used something like it to gain the sort of *agape* needed to allow their peace to come back upon them in the face of nasty treatment from others. Their mysticism also informed them as to when violence is necessary for the greater good, such as opposing a tyrant like Hitler. Goodness is a great goal to dedicate a life of journeying toward.

We need that vision of oneness to truly love. And loving all and always may be impossible for most of us. The Religion of Good doesn't make us saints. It only makes us human beings with a vision (and a flawed one, as I keep saying). It only refines us, but that refinement never stops. We will never solve the ethics crisis with love alone, because too few of us are sages.

However, our vision from our Religion of Good journey may well lead to love. It will be imperfect. Sometimes we probably will lash out at those who discourage us, but at least we'll know that may mean it's time to go on another journey. Love is still a great thing, indeed! May the Religion of Good guide and refine your love.

Now that we've reviewed all this, you may well point out that it's all well and good that we come to more and more individual ethical clarity in ourselves, but you still worry that the Religion of Good is just the sort of ideological black box we're trying to avoid. While it may help us better understand the source of our ethics, as well as how to refine it, it seems impossible to explain that derivation to anyone else, much less convince anyone else to share our ethical convictions.

The short answer is that this journey I'm suggesting builds synergy. Let me explain.

I've never been trying to persuade you of any ethics of my own. My goal with this book is not to reveal to society how we can agree on ethics, because I don't know the answer to that. In fact, I often wonder if our free society creates such a wide bell curve of ethical opinions (which is a good thing) that resolving them all in any final way is nigh impossible.

My primary goal has been to help us ethical individuals gain better insight into our ethical understandings, to refine our own inner goodness by our own light, and perhaps to adjust our ethics as our insights improve. But I think this process also has value to society as a whole, and I'm opposed to black boxes.

My secondary goal is actually to help us leave our black box ideologies and our echo chambers, not through common ethics but through common practices and through the virtues of humility, courage, and tolerance that must accompany them. When each of us come to our own ethical epiphanies, we can come together in better harmony in a pluralistic society.

I sometimes worry that our civilization is about to be torn apart. Somehow we manage to glue everything together so it doesn't, but I can't help feeling that our ships of state are on rocky waves in the deep ocean. There's a harmony that I believe we can find, though. By having better clarity into our own ethics, applying those ethics in our lives, and discussing our disparate values in a polite, honest, and honorable way, we begin to create social synergy.

It's not that our ethics converge. If our ethics do converge, within the open forum of a free society, that would be wonderful, but I'm not holding my breath. I also worry that a lot of factions are trying to solve this problem by imposing their *moralism* on everyone. So, I question whether we should really focus on ethical convergence right now.

By following my proposal, we gain better understandings of our ethical differences. In doing so, we become more aware of our own ideologies as well as those of others. Rather than taking our ethics to be absolute facts with which to bully others, we can understand ourselves as seeing, imperfectly, some sort of whole. This realization leads to another, which is that others are striving as strongly as we are to see that same whole.[4]

Even if we are all like the blind people with the elephant, it's good to admit that all the things the blind people are mistaking the elephant for (the snake, the rope, the wall, and so on) are in fact imperfect understandings. That is, it's good for us to see that other people with very different worldviews care as deeply about goodness as we do. They just see it differently.

There's an old Christian hymn by G. K. Chesterton that's been running through my head as I've been writing this book. *O God of earth and altar, Bow down and hear our cry. Our earthly rulers falter, Our people drift and die. The walls of gold entomb us, The swords of scorn divide. Take not thy thunder from us, But take away our pride.* Well, I believe in

---

4   There are undoubtedly bad actors, too. Not *everyone* is striving for good, but many people in different ideological camps from our own are striving for ethics in a way that we're ignorant of, and they're ignorant of our ethical strivings as well.

humility informed by self-esteem and good ego, but the point of the hymn is well taken.

Now, none of this is to say that we should tolerate authoritarian ideologies. The seduction of moralistic ideologies is that some aspects of them are moral. It's their authoritarian framework that corrupts them, and it's not worth having our free societies fall just to have the imperfect and often twisted moral systems that they seek to impose on us. Those of us who believe in liberty can and should make a stand against authoritarianism. Our ability to discuss ethics therefore requires the values of a free society.

Nor does it mean that we should all make nice. Our free society entails political debate. Democracy requires us to disagree boldly, if politely, in order to function. The public forum entails friction, even when we're all being polite. All this empowers us to see beyond authoritarian moralism (and rightly so). Maybe we exacerbate the ethics crisis by having the arrogance to think that our ideology is the right one. And, so, society fractures further, along moralistic fault lines.

That arrogance gives way when we use the Religion of Good to come to see a valuable but ever-flawed vision of goodness. We realize that we live among many fellows, each finding our own visions by transcending ourselves. In doing so, our individual souls arise as citizens of the cosmos, each equally responsible for the well-being of the commonwealth of all sentient beings.

Religion has traditionally had the role of supplying people with morals, but traditional organized religions may lead to more ideology, and thus more fracturing, unless they remember to stay within the bounds of a free society. Even then, they are in danger of failing to contribute to ethical synergy as long as they dig in their heals ideologically. Long-established religions can benefit from the Religion of Good, however, by using their own spiritual techniques to help each of the faithful develop a personal relationship with goodness.

When people in, say, a church find out that people in the synagogue or mosque down the street are going on the same transcendent journeys that they are taking, they can form a common bond around practice, if not values. Each of the religious in their respective religions can find respect for those of other religions, or of no religion at all, by seeing the same oneness from their own perspectives.

Philosophy has become the privilege of an erudite, esoteric, and increasingly remote elite. I love philosophy because it helps us think through hard issues, but even with my liberal arts education, I barely feel up to entering the philosophical forum among PhDs. However, by using the techniques of religion, in a not-so-traditional and less organized manner, ordinary people like you and me can find our own personal ethical epiphanies—without a PhD.[5]

By coming together with many ethical visions and comparing our notes, we gain a new vocabulary with which to discuss ethics. Remember when I advised you to write poetry or make art based on the visions you had on your journeys? That creative expression forms new ethical myths. Shared within a pluralistic culture, these myths join with older ones to form an alphabet by which we can refine our ethical language, and perhaps contribute to it, even with a bit of polite friction.

Telling you what morals to have would only fracture our society further. But by inviting us all to come together around the ongoing (if often contentious) interaction of ethical language, drawn ultimately from our own transcendence of ourselves, I'm asking us, as a society of individuals, to stop fracturing our ethical fabric and instead grow together, ethically, around a common set of techniques and an open salon in which we discuss our respective views of the Good.

This requires the virtues of tolerance, politeness, courage, and mercy. We have to be patient with each other and realize that none of us knows the truth. We have to be prepared to tell others what we think is right, only to have them reject it. We'll need to allow others to walk away from our ethical entreaties, unconvinced. But I have faith that the discussion will be fruitful.

Even if you remain unconvinced by another's ethics, having your ethics challenged will refine your soul. Likewise, your amicable discussions with others will give them insights into their own ethics. It will take aplomb to do all this. Fortunately, I believe that our transcendent journey to the Good will strengthen these virtues, because they all entail seeing us all together. In short, let's dance rather than fight!

A pluralistic society does not need more religions or more philosophies.[6] It needs to transcend still higher to a sort of meta-religion. This cannot be another ideology, but rather a proposal that affirms the freedom of all people to decide for themselves. The Neoplatonists of late antiquity spoke of *theurgy*—working of the Divine—as opposed to *theology*—talking about the Divine. The Religion of Good is, metaphorically, a sort of theurgy of the Good. It cannot be transmitted by any prophet, however, or it will degrade to more ideology—more social fracture.

This will need to come about through something more like ethical interfaith. It must be a practice that enables ethical individuals to come to individual conclusions about ethics, while still allowing

---

5 And all this can still be informed by philosophy and religion. The goal is not to replace these institutions, only to add to them.
6 To put it another way, new religions and philosophies should be ones that go toward solving, rather than exacerbating, the ethics crisis.

ethical dialog to take place within society. This dialog itself must be more or less good, and it must more or less invite goodness to arise within it, greater than the sum of its parts. This is the solution I'm proposing to the ethics crisis.

Appendix I: Recipes for Goodness

Here I've listed all the rituals in the body of this book, plus several more that you may find useful. Please feel free to photocopy or otherwise duplicate any of these, whether for personal use or use with your spiritual community. If you do so, please give appropriate attribution, and do not use this for commercial purposes. Also, please feel free to modify them to suit your personal needs or the needs of your spiritual group.

These instructions assume that you have an altar (or at least a makeshift altar) and that you have it looking the way you prefer (put an altar cloth over it, and so on.).

Some notes on format: I've italicized comments, to distinguish them from things you actually say. I've put anything you say out loud, like a chant, in bold upper case for easy reading. Everything else, such as instructions, a list of what you'll need, and so on, are normal (unitalicized *and not all caps).*

Recipe 1: A Meditation on Goodness
This is the meditation from the end of Chapter 1.

Find as much quiet as you can, but if cars honk outside your home, or neighbors yell, let that in. Take a minute to meditate on why there's so much badness in the world and how we can bring more good into it.

Recipe 2: Balancing Empathy, Self-Discipline, and Love

This is the exercise at the end of Chapter 3, which I offered as an example of working with the Tetractys. The goal is to balance empathy, self-discipline, and love, with love in the middle. Love is both a mediator between empathy and self-discipline and informed by them. As always, feel free to modify it.

What You'll Need:
1. Images of three angel figures of self-discipline, empathy, and love
2. Sandalwood (for self-discipline), rose (for love), and lavender incense (for empathy)
3. Three censers, or one censer that can hold three incense sticks
4. Matches or a lighter to light the incense
5. A bell (or a bell app on your phone, or something else to make noise—hands will do)
6. A cheat sheet with the following on it (write big or print out this page).

Self-Discipline Prayer:
>ANGEL OF SELF-DISCIPLINE,
>PLEASE HELP ME TO BE STRONG
>AND IN CONTROL OF MYSELF
>FOR THE GOOD OF ALL.

Compassion Prayer:
>ANGEL OF EMPATHY,
>PLEASE OPEN MY HEART TO FEEL
>FOR ALL SENTIENT BEINGS.

Love Prayer:
>ANGEL OF LOVE,
>PLEASE GUIDE ME TO BALANCE
>SELF-DISCIPLINE AND EMPATHY,
>GUIDED BY LOVE.

Chant:
>I MASTER MYSELF!
>I FEEL FOR MY FELLOWS!
>I LIVE IN LOVE!

Performing the Ritual

Be sure to have your cheat sheet handy, either on the altar, in your pocket, or the like, so you can read the prayers and the chant off it when the time comes.

1. Set the three angels on your altar, with the angel of love in the middle and the angels of self-discipline and empathy on either side.

2. Setup your three incense sticks so that, ideally, the sandalwood is in front of the self-discipline angel, the rose in front of the love angel, and the lavender in front of the empathy angel.

3. Take three deep breaths, breathing in cosmic energy, and breathing out negativity.

4. Walk around the ritual area ringing the bell.

5. Light the sandalwood incense and recite the Self-Discipline Prayer from your cheat sheet.

6. Light the lavender incense and recite the Empathy Prayer.

7. Light the rose incense and recite the Love Prayer.

8. Begin chanting the Chant. Continue chanting it until you feel that you are done.

9. Walk around the ritual area one more time, ringing the bell.

10. Bow to the angels to conclude the ritual.

Recipe 3: A Meditation on the Material World

This is the meditation at the end of Chapter 4, "Taking Stock in the Material World".

What You'll Need:
You don't really need anything for this, but a bell is nice.

Performing the Meditation

1. Take three deep breaths. With each in-breath, draw in power from the world around you. With each out-breath, breathe all doubts and unnecessary thoughts and feelings into the earth. Ring the bell.

2. Focus on this world, with all its imperfections.

3. Focus on yourself. How do you feel in body, mind, and heart? Do you feel part of this world or stranger in it?

4. Affirm that you're a part of it and you belong here.

5. Focus on the good of this world, the good of others, and your own goodness.

6. Accept this world, and feel your power to act in it, acknowledging that there will be things in it you cannot change.

7. Focus on your ethics about how to use your power.

8. Breath power into yourself.

9. Take another deep breath and end your meditation with a ringing of the bell.

Recipe 4: Ritual of Lady Liberty

This is the liberty ritual from Chapter 6. Parts of it draw on material written by Valerie Voigt for the Waxing Moon Tradition of Wicca, used with permission.

What You'll Need
1. A bowl of water
2. A container of salt
3. A censer to burn incense
4. Incense in the censer
5. Matches or a lighter to light the incense
6. A small replica or image of the Statue of Liberty (a printout from the internet is fine)
7. OPTIONAL: A bell
8. OPTIONAL: A fan to fan the incense

Grounding
1. Sit or stand comfortably.
2. Take three deep breaths. With each breath, breathe in cosmic energy, hold for a moment, then breathe negative emotions into the earth. You can pick your negative emotions back up after the ritual, if you still need them.
3. Feel that you are a tree.
4. Send your roots deep down into the earth.
5. Draw up the moisture, nutrients, and power of Mother Earth.
6. Feel it rise up your spine.
7. Reach your fingers up above your head, like branches.
8. Say,
   I AM HERE. I AM HERE. I AM HERE.

Purification
1. Touch your hand to the bowl of water and say,
   I CONJURE WATER!
2. Touch your hand to the salt container and say,
   I CONJURE EARTH!
3. Take three pinches of salt and mix it with the water in the bowl, saying,
   TOGETHER, THEY ARE THE WOMB.
4. Sprinkle yourself, anyone else in the ritual, and the space with the salt water, working your way around the room clockwise. If you have anything in the room that shouldn't get wet, you may want to just go through the motions, without actually sprinkling water on it.
5. As you sprinkle, visualize white light clearing away all negativity.

Blessing
1. Light the incense. (Obviously, be careful not to set anything else on fire.) Pick up the fan, if you're using one. Say,
   I CONJURE FIRE!
2. Blow out the incense and say,
   I CONJURE AIR!
   TOGETHER, THEY ARE THE SPARK OF LIFE.
3. Wave the incense smoke over you, anyone else in the ritual, and the place you're holding the ritual, again moving in a clockwise fashion around the area.
4. As you do so, visualize sunlight blessing the area with goodness.

Beginning Sacred Time and Creating Sacred Space
1. Walk around the ritual area three times, ringing the bell.
2. As you do so, chant,
   CIRCLE! CIRCLE! ROUND ABOUT!
   POWER STAY IN AND WORLD STAY OUT!
3. When you come back to the altar, ring the bell one more time before setting it back down.

Recreating the Cosmos
1. Face east and say,
   HAIL TO SPIRITS OF THE EAST.
   If you prefer, you can say, "angels" instead of "spirits."
2. Repeat this for south, west, and north, so that you salute each direction, going around clockwise from east to north.

Call on Lady Liberty
1. If you are performing the ritual with others, stand in a circle and join hands. If by yourself, face the Statue of Liberty on your altar.
2. Say,
   LADY LIBERTY! PRAISE BE TO THEE!
   HELP US TAKE RESPONSIBILITY FOR OUR FREEDOM.
   HELP US GROW FROM INDIVIDUALS TO CITIZENS,
   FROM CITIZENS OF SOCIETIES
       TO CITIZENS OF THE COSMOS,
   EACH TO STEER THE SHIP OF STATE.
3. Bow.

Doing the Work
1. If you are working with others, hold hands in a circle. Otherwise, stand in front of the altar, facing the center of the area.

2. Start chanting,
FREEDOM! O, FREEDOM! FOR GOOD AND FOR ALL!
3. Continue to chant as you dance in a circle, clockwise. If you can't dance, due to disability or the like, you can just sit or stand and chant. If you're in a group and one or more of your members is too disabled to dance, invite them to sit, provide them with a chair and a rhythm instrument to play during the dance, or invite them to clap if you don't have an instrument.
4. Keep dancing until you feel you're done, perhaps three to seven rounds.
5. If you know you won't disturb anybody with the noise, give a big whoop or ululation at the end to really shoot your chant off like fireworks on Fourth of July.

Or, if you're not American, pick a visualization that makes sense to you.

Thanking Lady Liberty
1. Once again join hands, if in a group, or face your Statue of Liberty, if it's just you.
2. Say,

LADY LIBERTY. THANK YOU FOR YOUR ATTENTION AND YOUR BLESSING IN THIS RITE. YOU ARE WITH US ALWAYS.

Releasing the Cosmos
1. Face north. Say,

HAIL TO THE NORTH! THANK YOU FOR YOUR BLESSING ON THIS RITE. FAREWELL!

2. Do the same for west, south, and east, such that you say farewell to each direction in a counterclockwise manner.

Decommissioning Sacred Space and Ending Sacred Time
1. Walk counterclockwise around the ritual area three times, ringing the bell.
2. As you do so, chant,

WORK DONE! WEB SPUN! CIRCLE END WHERE 'TWAS BEGUN.

3. When you return to the altar, ring the bell one last time, before setting it back down.

Grounding Again
1. Kneel down.
2. Touch your head to the ground.
3. Feel any remaining "energy" from the ritual go into the earth.

After the ritual, I suggest doing something fun, enjoying your freedom.

Recipe 5: Ritual of Oneness

This is the ritual from Chapter 8, "The Journey up the Tetractys." I suggest using this as your general purpose ritual for general insight into goodness, and using the others to focus on certain subjects.

Some of this paraphrases the Esbat ritual of Waxing Moon tradition of Wicca. The Purification, Blessing, Creating the Cosmos, and Releasing the Cosmos sections closely paraphrase ceremonial material written by Valerie Voigt. Her purification and charging material was in turn inspired by a spoken chant by Sally Eaton. My wording is used with their permission.

What You'll Need
1. An altar or makeshift altar, optionally covered with an altar cloth
2. A bowl of water
3. A container of salt
4. An incense censer
5. Incense in the censer
6. Matches or a lighter
7. A hand-drawn picture of people holding hands in a circle, at the crossroads, with Mother Earth in the middle. Actually draw this yourself, to put your personal "energy" into the ritual. Place it on the altar, or in the center of the circle, if you're performing this as a group.

Grounding
Sit or stand comfortably. Close your eyes. Visualize yourself as a tree. See your roots going deep into the earth. Reach your hands above your head, spreading your fingers. Reach these, your "branches" up to the sky. Say,
> **I AM HERE. I AM HERE. I AM HERE.**

Purification
1. Touch your hand to the bowl of water and say,
   THE WATERS OF INTUITION!
2. Touch your hand to the salt container and say,
   THE SALT OF THE EARTH!
3. Take three pinches of salt and mix it with the water in the bowl.
4. Sprinkle the salt water on yourself and the area. As you do, chant,
   **BY WATER AND EARTH, FULL ONCE AROUND,
   IN THE NAME OF THE ALL,
   I HALLOW THIS GROUND.
   BEFORE IT MUST ALL EVIL FLEE.
   THIS IS MY WILL! SO MOTE IT BE!**

Blessing
1. Touch the censer. Say,
   THE AIR OF CLARITY.
2. Light the incense. (Obviously, be careful not to set anything else on fire.) Say,
   THE FIRE OF WILL.
3. Pick up the fan, if you're using one. Wave the incense smoke over you, anyone else in the ritual, and the place you're holding the ritual, again moving in a clockwise fashion around the area. As you do so, visualize sunlight blessing the area with goodness. Wave the incense over yourself and the area you'll be performing the ritual in. Chant,
   BY FIRE AND AIR, FULL ONCE AROUND,
   IN THE NAME OF THE ONE,
   I HALLOW THIS GROUND.
   BEFORE IT MUST ALL EVIL FLEE.
   THIS IS MY WILL! SO MOTE IT BE!

Beginning Sacred Time and Creating Sacred Space
Walk around the area, ringing the bell, and chanting,
   CIRCLE, CIRCLE, ROUND ABOUT
   WITH ONE AND ALL THROUGHOUT AND ABOUT.

Recreating the Cosmos
1. Face east and say,
   ANGELS OF THE RISING SUN,
   BRIGHTEN MY SOUL TO KNOW THE GOOD.
2. Face south and say,
   ANGELS OF THE WARM SOUTH,
   EMBLAZEN MY WILL TO WORK THE GOOD.
3. Face west and say,
   ANGELS OF THE SETTING SUN,
   EMBOLDEN MY HEART TO SEE THE GOOD.
4. Face north and say,
   ANGELS OF THE COLD NORTH,
   QUIET MY MIND TO RECEIVE THE GOOD.

Call on Mother Earth
Chant three times through,
   MOTHER EARTH BLUE AND GREEN,
   GLOBAL GIRTH AND CROSSROAD QUEEN.
Bow to honor Mother Earth.

The Chant of Oneness
Chant the following over and over again until your mind goes blank. Or else continue for at least a good long while; maybe fifteen minutes minimum.
> **I AM WE.**
> **WE ARE ONE.**
> **WE ARE ONE**
> **AND I AM WE.**

Thanking Mother Earth
Bow to the image of Mother Earth, and say,
> **MOTHER EARTH, THANK YOU FOR YOUR BLESSING.**
> **YOU ARE WITH US ALWAYS.**

Releasing the Cosmos
Face North and say,
> **ANGELS OF THE COLD NORTH,**
> **THANK YOU FOR YOUR BLESSING.**

Face West and say,
> **ANGELS OF THE SETTING SUN,**
> **THANK YOU FOR YOUR BLESSING.**

Face South and say,
> **ANGELS OF THE WARM SOUTH,**
> **THANK YOU FOR YOUR BLESSING.**

Face East and say,
> **ANGELS OF THE RISING SUN,**
> **THANK YOU FOR YOUR BLESSING.**

Decommissioning Sacred Space and Time
Go counterclockwise around the space, ringing the bell, while chanting,
> **WORK DONE! WEB SPUN!**
> **CIRCLE END WHERE 'TWAS BEGUN.**

Perform the tree visualization a second time, to ground again.

A Daily Practice Version

Once you've become so proficient at this ritual that you have it in you, as it were, you might consider also doing it as a daily practice to make it go down deep.

To do so ...

1. Take three deep breaths, breathing in cosmic energy and breathing negativity down into the earth.

2. Ring the bell.

3. Chant for at least five minutes,
   I AM WE.
   WE ARE ONE.
   WE ARE ONE
   AND I AM WE.

4. Take one more deep breath and finish.

Recipe 6: Taking Stock of Yourself

Here's a practice that is not in the body of the book, but I think it's good to do. The basic idea is to observe your mind. This is good for all sorts of things.

It's good to know what's going on inside of ourselves in order to be our best selves. We all know how we can create our own illusions to cloud our minds and make us do things, even when we think those things are wrong. We can also fail to see important things that we need to attend to. It can be good just to keep track of what's going on in our minds. We can't focus on every aspect of our mind throughout our busy day. So it's good to take stock, keep ourselves honest about ourselves, and be sure we know what's going on with us. That's all part of being a good person.

You might think of this as stock keeping in a store, or doing the books. If you're going to run a business effectively, you have to know how much you're spending, how much you owe, and how much income you're receiving. Likewise, to run a good mind, you have to know what's passing through it.

To a large extent, the following ritual has been influenced by my Zen Buddhist upbringing, and the meditation in the middle will be recognizable as such. But I also like to put some ritual around it, so I've brought in the Wiccan-ish sort of ritual that should be familiar to you by now.

In Buddhism, there's the historical Buddha who founded it (often called Gautama Buddha because his surname was Gautama, or just the Buddha), but Buddhists speak of many Buddhas, because there is the potential for all sentient beings to become enlightened. So I've used both images of Buddhas, in the plural, and the Buddha, in the singular.

I'll also note that by now many of these rituals should look similar to you. Some portions—the parts at the beginning and end that set it up, create sacred space, and take it down—are the same as or similar to the others. Feel free to use this pattern in designing your own rituals.

What You'll Need
Nothing is strictly necessary for this, though the meditation cushion is practical.
1. A Buddha statue or image
2. A bowl of water
3. A container of salt
4. An incense censer
5. Incense in the censer—I prefer sandalwood for this, but your mileage may vary
6. Matches or a lighter
7. A meditation cushion or some other comfortable seat
8. a bell
9. a journal

Grounding

Sit or stand comfortably. Close your eyes. Visualize yourself as a tree. See your roots going deep into the earth. Reach your hands above your head, spreading your fingers. Reach these, your "branches," up to the sky. Say,
> **I AM HERE. I AM HERE. I AM HERE.**

Purification

Touch the water bowl. Say,
> **THE WATERS OF INTUITION.**

Touch the salt box. Say,
> **THE SALT OF THE EARTH.**

Mix a few pinches of salt into the water in the bowl.
Sprinkle the salt water on yourself and the area. As you do, chant,
> **BY WATER AND EARTH, FULL ONCE AROUND,**
> **IN THE NAME OF THE ALL,**
> **I HALLOW THIS GROUND.**
> **BEFORE IT MUST ALL EVIL FLEE.**
> **THIS IS MY WILL! SO MOTE IT BE!**

Blessing

Touch the censer. Say,
> **THE AIR OF CLARITY.**

Light the incense. Say,
> **THE FIRE OF WILL**

Wave the incense over yourself and the area you'll be performing the ritual in. Chant,
> **BY FIRE AND AIR, FULL ONCE AROUND,**
> **IN THE NAME OF THE ONE,**
> **I HALLOW THIS GROUND.**
> **BEFORE IT MUST ALL EVIL FLEE.**
> **THIS IS MY WILL! SO MOTE IT BE!**

Beginning Sacred Time and Creating Sacred Space

Walk around the area, ringing the bell, and chanting,
> **CIRCLE, CIRCLE, ROUND ABOUT**
> **WITH ONE AND ALL THROUGHOUT AND ABOUT**

Recreating the Cosmos

Face east and say,
> **BUDDHAS OF THE RISING SUN,**
> **BRIGHTEN MY SOUL TO KNOW THE GOOD.**

Face south and say,
> **BUDDHAS OF THE WARM SOUTH,**
> **EMBLAZEN MY WILL TO WORK THE GOOD.**

Face west and say,
> BUDDHAS OF THE SETTING SUN,
> EMBOLDEN MY HEART TO SEE THE GOOD.

Face north and say,
> BUDDHAS OF THE COLD NORTH,
> QUIET MY MIND TO RECEIVE THE GOOD.

Calling the Buddha
> SIDDHARTHA GAUTAMA BUDDHA.
> PLEASE HELP ME TO KNOW MYSELF.

Meditation on Oneself
Sit comfortably. Breathe in and out, slowly, several times. Ring your bell. Allow your mind to become still, like a lake whose ripples subside. Look deep into your mind. See what's there. Just observe, without acting, judging, or responding too much. How do you feel? What thoughts are going through your head? Just take stock. When you're done, if you have a journal, jot some notes down about what's going on with your mind today.

Thanking the Characters
SIDDHARTHA GAUTAMA BUDDHA, THANK YOU FOR YOUR WISDOM.

Releasing the Cosmos
Face north and say,
> BUDDHAS OF THE COLD NORTH,
> THANK YOU FOR YOUR BLESSING.

Face west and say,
> BUDDHAS OF THE SETTING SUN,
> THANK YOU FOR YOUR BLESSING.

Face south and say,
> BUDDHAS OF THE WARM SOUTH,
> THANK YOU FOR YOUR BLESSING.

Face east and say,
> BUDDHAS OF THE RISING SUN,
> THANK YOU FOR YOUR BLESSING.

Decommissioning Sacred Space and Time
Go counterclockwise around the space ringing the bell, while chanting,
WORK DONE! WEB SPUN! CIRCLE END WHERE 'TWAS BEGUN.
Perform the tree visualization a second time, to ground again.

You can also do just the meditation, without all the ritual, and it will work just fine, as well. Doing it this way will make a good daily practice.

138   The Religion of Good

Recipe 7: Beauty Meditation

This is a meditation I created, but it's inspired by my Wiccan teaching. The "Charge of the Goddess," usually attributed to Doreen Valiente, which is perhaps the most recognized Wiccan text, references beauty several times. "I, who am the beauty of the green earth, and the white Moon among the stars, and the mystery of the waters, and the heart's desire, call unto thy soul ... let there be beauty and strength, power and compassion, honour and humility, mirth and reverence within you ... if that which thou seekest thou findest not within thee, thou wilt never find it without thee ... for behold, I have been with thee from the beginning; and I am that which is attained at the end of desire."

In my reading, the Charge says (1) that the Goddess is the beauty of nature and our hearts' desire (among other things), (2) the Goddess entreats us to find beauty in ourselves, and (3) the Goddess says that She is within us as well as without us. Therefore, our beauty is Her beauty.

This meditation is not meant to be factually or logically true. It is a practice that is meant to help us expand our love for the cosmos and possibly Divinity, as well as for our love for ourselves, as both reflections of Divinity and part of the cosmos. We are continuous with the cosmos. There is no point at which I end and the air begins, or the air ends and another person begins. When I invite you to say, in the meditation, "One with the cosmos," I'm invoking this concept of continuousness, as well as inviting you to realize that you are a reflection of the Divine. (And if you don't believe in the Divine, the practice will still work. Just think of it as poetry about your relationship to the cosmos and the beauty of existence.)

I usually put ten minutes on the timer when I do this exercise, which is ample time. Otherwise, I might take a walk around my neighborhood and make that a walking meditation, while I think the words in my head. Do the following over and over again until either the timer goes off or you're finished with your walk.

Inhale, then say,
   THE COSMOS IS BEAUTIFUL.

Exhale, then say,
   I'M BEAUTIFUL.

Inhale, then say,
   ONE WITH ...

Exhale, then say,
   ... THE COSMOS

Recipes 8+: Rituals of Virtues

You can take any virtue you like and build a ritual around it. The following is meant as a template for this. Simply supply the virtue. Common virtues might include: Love, Compassion, Self-Discipline, Mercy, Justice, Courage, Patience, Liberty, Tolerance, and Understanding. I've also written a list of virtues for a free society in Appendix IV, which this ritual could work with. This is, again, modeled closely after the Ritual of Oneness, with the just the middle swapped out.

What You'll Need
1. An altar or makeshift altar, optionally covered with an altar cloth
2. A bowl of water
3. A container of salt
4. An incense censer
5. Incense in the censer
6. Matches or a lighter
7. A symbol of the virtue

By now you should be proficient in coming up with such a symbol.

Grounding
Sit or stand comfortably. Close your eyes. Visualize yourself as a tree. See your roots going deep into the earth. Reach your hands above your head, spreading your fingers. Reach these, your "branches," up to the sky. Say,
> I AM HERE. I AM HERE. I AM HERE.

Purification
Touch the water bowl. Say,
> **THE WATERS OF INTUITION.**

Touch the salt box. Say,
> **THE SALT OF THE EARTH**

Mix a few pinches of salt into the water in the bowl.
Sprinkle the salt water on yourself and the area. As you do, chant,
> **BY WATER AND EARTH, FULL ONCE AROUND,**
> **IN THE NAME OF THE ALL,**
> **I HALLOW THIS GROUND.**
> **BEFORE IT MUST ALL EVIL FLEE.**
> **THIS IS MY WILL! SO MOTE IT BE!**

Blessing
Touch the censer. Say,
> **THE AIR OF CLARITY.**

Light the incense. Say,
> **THE FIRE OF WILL.**

Wave the incense over yourself and the area you'll be performing the ritual in. Chant,
> **BY FIRE AND AIR, FULL ONCE AROUND,**
> **IN THE NAME OF THE ONE,**
> > **I HALLOW THIS GROUND.**
> **BEFORE IT MUST ALL EVIL FLEE**
> **THIS IS MY WILL! SO MOTE IT BE!**

Beginning Sacred Time and Creating Sacred Space
Walk around the area, ringing the bell, and chanting,
> **CIRCLE, CIRCLE, ROUND ABOUT**
> **WITH ONE AND ALL THROUGHOUT AND ABOUT.**

Recreating the Cosmos
Face east and say,
> **ANGELS OF THE RISING SUN,**
> **BRIGHTEN MY SOUL TO KNOW THE GOOD.**

Face south and say,
> **ANGELS OF THE WARM SOUTH,**
> **EMBLAZEN MY WILL TO WORK THE GOOD.**

Face west and say,
> **ANGELS OF THE SETTING SUN,**
> **EMBOLDEN MY HEART TO SEE THE GOOD.**

Face north and say,
> **ANGELS OF THE COLD NORTH,**
> **QUIET MY MIND TO RECEIVE THE GOOD.**

Calling [Virtue]
You can use this call as a default, or write one specific to your virtue.
Chant three times through,
> **[VIRTUE], O [VIRTUE], DWELL WITH ME HERE!**

The Chant
You can also write your own chant, but here's a default.
Chant the name of the virtue over and over again until your mind goes blank.
> *You can also just put fifteen minutes on the timer, if you prefer.*

[VIRTUE], O [VIRTUE]!

Thanking the Virtue
[VIRTUE], THANK YOU FOR YOUR BLESSING.
YOU ARE WITH US ALWAYS.

Releasing the Cosmos
Face north and say,
ANGELS OF THE COLD NORTH,
THANK YOU FOR YOUR BLESSING.

Face west and say,
ANGELS OF THE SETTING SUN,
THANK YOU FOR YOUR BLESSING.

Face south and say,
ANGELS OF THE WARM SOUTH,
THANK YOU FOR YOUR BLESSING.

Face east and say,
ANGELS OF THE RISING SUN,
THANK YOU FOR YOUR BLESSING.

Decommissioning Sacred Space and Time
Go counterclockwise around the space ringing the bell, while chanting,
WORK DONE! WEB SPUN! CIRCLE END WHERE 'TWAS BEGUN.

Perform the tree visualization a second time, to ground again.

An Additional Thought

These recipes should generally help you, but sometimes life smacks us down so hard that our ordinary spiritual practices fail to get us out of the pit we're in. I'm no mental health expert and I give no mental health or medical advice. That being said, I've found from personal experience that there are times when it's been useful to focus on myself when I get plunged into that pit. I may just need to set aside a day for myself, do things I love, and find things to laugh about. Other times, I may need to fill my mind with affirmations, like *I love myself, I'm good enough*, and so forth. I may even develop chants or whole rituals around this. Doing all this pulls me out of that pit and gets me back to where I was before.

All things in moderation, though. I've found that if I focus on myself for too much longer than I really need, I can become egotistical, even uncompassionate. Once I'm out of the pit, I'll transition back to more typical spiritual practices, like the ones above, opening my heart again to love and to see the beauty of the cosmos and of other people. I just offer this thought, in case my personal experience with this is useful to you in the dark times of your life.

Daily Practice

You've probably noticed that I provided several daily practice versions of the rituals and practices above. There are different paths. For some, grand rituals less frequently (once a week or once a month) may be best. I've found that a daily practice in addition to these is best for me. For some, the daily practice may be most important. Developing a routine is essential for spiraling up. Any of these rituals can be converted to daily practices and for many that will be essential to making progress with fine-tuning their ethical intuition.

Appendix II:
Creating a Personal Place of Worship

It can be a great blessing to have a personal place where you can practice in your home. How you set it up, how large it is, where it is in the home, and how you decorate it are all personal choices. Here, I'll offer some thoughts that I hope you'll find useful.

At my home, I converted one of the bedrooms into a dedicated temple room. With a little help from my friends, I was able to get the walls painted in a bright orangish yellow and the ceiling in a twilight blue, all in ecological paint. My friends also helped me install soundproofing so as not to disturb my neighbors with my rituals. Thanks to everyone who worked on that!

I put in several altars for the various types of practices I do. I co-run two different micro-congregations out of my home. One is the Temple of Inanna and Dumuzi, a Mesopotamian Pagan temple. The other is Waxing Moon Circle, which is the original coven of the Waxing Moon tradition. I also have an altar just for myself.

I use the closet to store incense, candles, essential oils, and everything else that we need for our various activities. I lined one wall with bookshelves for my spiritual library. I also put in an ottoman bench that has storage for cushions that people can sit on. The bench doubles as sitting space for anyone who needs to sit during a ritual or meditation.

You don't have to do anything that elaborate (or maybe you'll come up with something more elaborate). Several things strike me as significant. First, I made the space my own. There's something very satisfying about making your own mark on a space, rather than just leaving it the way whatever corporation built your home made it.

This will probably be more difficult in a rented space (I own a condo), since you may need to get permission from your landlord or landlady. However, there are lots of ways one can make a space one's own. You could throw down a colorful throw rug. You can put art up on the walls. Making it your own is a step toward making it sacred. Once it's established, you might want to perform a ritual to consecrate it.

Secondly, it's a space set apart. The rest of my condo looks like a normal condo, but you can tell as soon as you enter it that my temple room is a special space. You don't have to do anything nearly as elaborate as a full room. It might just be a corner of an existing room. Maybe just put an altar in it. Decorate that with an altar cloth or what have you.

Some people I know create an outdoor space, too. You could have an outdoor altar, as long as it will either be okay in inclement weather or you take it down during bad weather. A fire pit can be nice. People naturally want to congregate around fires. You might want to mark sacred space with a circle of stones or something similar. These need not be big or expensive. They could be very simple and inexpensive.

The important thing is to have a space set aside for spiritual practice, however small it may be. It's okay to use it for other things. There's nothing wrong with having friends over for a barbecue in the same outdoor space you have set aside for spiritual work. They don't even have to know that that's what it is. They'll just think it's pretty.

Several things make sacred space. One is the demarcation of the boundary. In my temple room, this is accomplished by painting the walls. In an outdoor space with a circle of stones, the stone circle accomplishes this. In a portion of a room, screens can be used to demarcate space, as can a throw rug that forms the floor just of that space, or furniture arranged to set the space off.

Having an entrance is important, too. In my temple room, this is the door. In an outdoor space, this might simply be a gap in the stones, flanked by some stones that are a little different than the others. The point is that people who enter it should feel that they've stepped over some threshold into someplace special.

The third thing that makes a space sacred is what's in it. It should contain sacred and only sacred things pertinent to the activities to be done in it. I recommend keeping your symbol kit here as well as any notes on rituals and ritual supplies. This might include things like angel or Buddha statues, incense, bells, matches, and a notebook to keep notes on rituals.

It's okay to have practical things like brooms and dustpans. I consider those to be sacred if they're set aside for cleaning my temple room. The point is that the sacred space should not be used for non-sacred purposes. (The barbecue I mentioned earlier is an exception in my mind, because there's something inherently sacred about people coming together to eat around a cooking fire). As far as cleaning goes, I also recommend keeping your sacred space clean and ready for use.

In the end, though, it's up to you. A sacred area could be small or large, indoor or outdoor. It could be just an altar and a meditation cushion in the corner of a bedroom. That's all fine. The most important thing is that anyone in it (most particularly you) should feel that it's set aside for spiritual purposes.

Appendix III:
Co-creating a Circle of Imperfect Peers

It's fine to practice by yourself, but it can be helpful to practice with others, for a variety of reasons. First, we're social creatures and even the most introverted of us (like me) have a need for social contact. Secondly, we may want to keep ourselves honest and reasonably humble (non-arrogant while still possessing a healthy self-esteem). Practicing with others reminds us that we're not saints, just people. Thirdly, practicing with others allows us to bounce ideas off of our peers and be sounding boards for them, in return.

I think the starting point in establishing a group is the word *peer*. The goal is to assemble a group of rough equals, rather than a hierarchy. For our purposes, I think a hierarchy is contraindicated. In some spiritual paths, a teacher/student relationship is appropriate, but that's not what I'm talking about here. Remember that our experience of the Good in the Monad is ineffable. Thinking that our insights are somehow superior to those of others tends to lead in a toxic, cultish direction. Dangerous cults fail to serve humanity and increase the infighting of ideologies.[1] So I urge you to avoid hierarchies.

It may be, however, that you're at the center of a group. That's why I call it a *circle*. Like the Knights of the Round Table, you will each be peers, each helping the others. But there will probably be one person or more who establishes the circle. This person—or people—may emerge as organizers. The important thing is to distinguish between administrative leadership and a concept of spiritual advancement. I think it's inevitable that some people will be more central to the administration of a group. The difference is that I'd avoid any thought of "spiritual elitism". I think that will detract from your goals.

Speaking of which, if you're the founder or co-founder of a little circle, you might write up a mission statement outlining some of this (like the concept that no one members is more "enlightened" than another). Once the circle gets established and is operating well, I'd

---

[1] There are two different meanings of the word *cult* that I should clarify. The word *cult* comes from a Latin word that simply meant the body of worship around a particular deity or group of deities. That's still how academics, like classicists, use it today. In common parlance, we use the word to mean the dangerous type of cult where you wouldn't want to drink the Kool-Aid. Dangerous or toxic cults are ones in which the leader or leaders manipulate members for their own gain, such as manipulating them into sex, taking their money (or even all their earthly possessions), or even using members as virtual slaves for free labor. The late Isaac Bonewits, who was in life a modern Druid, created a simple test to determine if you're dealing with a dangerous cult. This is the Advanced Bonewits Cult Danger Evaluation Frame (or ABCDEF), which you can find online here: http://www.neopagan.net/ABCDEF.html

also suggest encouraging other long-term members to take on administrative tasks. It can be a burden on a founder or co-founder to always be the one holding the bag. It can be healthy to make administrative roles ones that members rotate through. It will tend to mitigate hierarchy, so no one person is complaining that they do "all the work."

You might make a list of roles. Maybe one person is in charge of stock keeping for things such as incense and candles. Another person might be in charge of managing contacts and communications. This might include getting the word out to members when you're all meeting and for what purpose. Maybe others might be in charge of keeping the sacred space clean. You may also want to meet at different members' locations each time, so that it's not always on one person to play host or hostess.

Don't be afraid to start small and remain relatively small. In fact, I think that's best. After your first journey, it can be easy to be so full of zeal that you go out and make a public social media group. However, that might be too much too soon. The purpose of a group is mutual support, not "spreading the good word." In my experience, growing too fast can sometimes get some undesirable people. Unfortunately, they exist, so don't be naïve. Instead, you might start with friends that you're reading this book with. Start out with people you know and trust, and whom you know to be reliable.

I would also keep money to a minimum. Too much money in these sorts of things tends to move the group in the direction of a dangerous cult. Instead, I'd focus on making sure everything that's needed for each meeting is on hand. This would include whatever is used in each ritual as well as things like food to eat during social time. One strategy is to have different people responsible for purchasing the actual items. Arrange refreshments either as a potluck or the responsibility of a rotating host or hostess. That way you don't need to keep track of monies.

The problem with money is that someone always has to control it. Some people may be able to donate more. When my initiating High Priestess, Valerie Voigt, and I teach Wicca classes together, we require all our students to pay it forward through community service and to chip in on supplies.

A student once asked us if she could just give money to charity and give us cash so we could buy supplies. Because we knew her to be pretty well off, we said no, on the grounds that she would have been using money to get out of community activities. Actually working in a soup kitchen, for example, is a very different experience of service than just giving money to the soup kitchen. You actually have the experience of interacting with homeless people. Actually buying incense and bringing it by class does more to contribute to the community than just giving the teachers money to buy the incense. You actually experience the effort that goes into stocking a spiritual space. When money is involved, the organization can start becoming about the money rather than about spirituality.

I'd also keep politics out. One major goal of working on the Religion of Good with others is to expose yourself to different conceptions of goodness, rather than to allow ourselves to stay in the echo chambers of our minds thinking that we know best. How do the blind people figure out that the elephant is an elephant? They compare notes. Likewise, we want to explore the Good mutually, and that entails learning about other people's perspectives on it.

Politics will only distract you. If you're members of different parties, movements, or factions, no matter how good you are as human beings, it's too easy to demonize other people for their political affiliations. People have political alignments for many reasons. Just because other people are members of different political parties or movements from you does not automatically mean that they endorse repugnant or morally bankrupt candidates or ideas. As I talk to a politically diverse population, I'm surprised to find goodness everywhere. I've come to realize that I share a great deal ethically with people of all different political and religious persuasions. What I find most heartening about encountering political diversity, in the context of our human quest for ethics, is the fact that we're all searching for what's good. Even if we disagree, I know my very different fellow travelers have good hearts.

Remember, too, that we no longer have one source of truth in the news media. We have a variety of biases, all vying for power, most of them corporate. We have become a society of echo chambers. None of us knows if we're in an echo chamber, because anyone who's in one typically needs an outsider just to observe that it *is* an echo chamber. I guarantee you that, even if a fellow traveler supports a politician you find repugnant (and who may indeed *be* repugnant), the news media your fellow traveler is exposed to are presenting that candidate through rosy-tinted lenses that obscure that candidate's ugliness. Your fellow traveler may still be a very good-hearted, well-meaning person. Even if someone's ideas are really weird, they may be in an echo chamber—or perhaps just a different echo chamber from the one you're in. Try to remember that we're all victims of corporate news media. We're not coming together to fight. We're coming together to seek goodness.

Moreover, one key virtue we're trying to nurture in ourselves is tolerance for diverse ethical opinions, so that we can live synergistically in an ethically pluralistic society. We have many cultures, many individuals, and quite a few mavericks all living together, and we have to get along. Tolerance of ethical diversity is a virtue that is all important in our quest to gain insight and wisdom into goodness. Treat ethical diversity as an opportunity to grow as a person rather than something to avoid. This is really the only alternative to civil war.

The more you can keep everything friendly, small, intimate, and amateur, the better. If your group is a small one that will fit comfortably within the space of a living room, you'll probably have an organic little group that will function well, just by everyone being friendly and polite. If a circle gets much bigger than that, I'd recommend having it split, rather than trying to accommodate dozens of people. It won't work as well, anyway, because it's hard for too many people to share their experiences, particularly if everything is supposed to happen on a peer-to-peer basis.

Appendix IV:
The Virtues of a Free Society

In the body of this book, I have chosen not to talk about my own ethics, because that's not the point. I want each of us to figure out ethics for ourselves and then put our heads together and see if we can agree on some things. What I want to avoid is ideology wars. If I weigh in, I might be contributing to ideological schisms.

There *is* something I think that we should nail down, however, and that's the values of a free society itself. If the practice I'm recommending is going to work, we all need to respect one another's ethical views. If we're going to have an ethically pluralistic society, we need guidelines to circumscribe all of that in order to have rules of thumb for how we discuss diverse ideas in a peaceful way. The only alternative would seem to be civil war.

So I've been thinking a lot about how we can best coexist within ethical pluralism. The problem is that ideologues share their reasoning much less often than do those of us who share our ethical thoughts sincerely, bravely, and in a way that is respectful of ethical diversity. I worry that we've forgotten how to dialogue respectfully. I feel every day that people put their own ideologies before the values of a free society and that our sacred public forums have devolved into shouting matches.

In researching this book, I read two books by Alasdair MacIntyre: *A Short History of Ethics* and *After Virtue*. In these (and particularly in *After Virtue*), MacIntyre argues for bringing something called *teleology* back into the philosophical debate on ethics. Teleology is the study not just of how things in nature change but of how they *ought* to change—for example, how we *ought* to mature as human beings. It's a concept that comes to us from the virtue ethics of antiquity, through philosophers such as Aristotle, but it has been set aside in modern times.

The reason is that biologists urge us to *avoid* a teleological understanding of evolution: the idea that there's something we're *supposed* to be evolving into rather than the idea that we're just changing. A teleological understanding of evolution tends to lead to things like eugenics and social Darwinism, which are things I hope most of us want to avoid.

However, that's not the only kind of teleology you can have. MacIntyre enumerates different ones in different eras. In the era of Homer, the teleology of how a nobleman grew into a warrior was important. In the classical period of ancient Greece, what mattered was growing into being a good citizen of the *polis*. In medieval Christian Europe, it was growing into being a good Christian, and so on.

MacIntyre points out that different teleologies imply different sets of virtues. Teleology takes human beings from how we are by nature to how we are once our nature has been informed by our *telos* (Greek for *purpose*). So, any given teleology implies point A and point B. How do we get from one to another? MacIntyre's answer is that any given teleology implies certain virtues: to become a warrior, you must attain warrior virtues; to become a citizen of a city state, you must attain civic virtues; to become a good Christian, you must attain Christian virtues.

That led me to think about what virtues are needed to maintain a free society. So I've been thinking that we should revive old Enlightenment ideas about common ethics around the public forum. Of course, all antiques need to be refurbished. Just so, the old seventeenth- and eighteenth-century philosophy that underpins it is worth seeing in a fresh, twenty-first-century light.[1]

I'm no philosopher. I'm just a priest of an obscure religion with a BA in Greco-Roman classics. What I'm about to present is not meant to be philosophy. It's not nearly rigorous enough for that. It's merely meant to show my train of thought as a citizen of a free society. As an educated person, I can still draw on philosophy to help us make sense of things.

The ethical thoughts I'd like to present do not form a complete ethical system. This is by design (as well as by the inability of anyone to form one that really works). My goal in thinking about ethics is to tease out the circumscribing ethics that allow for ethical pluralism to exist harmoniously.

I know I've argued against using reason to figure everything out about ethics. Instead, I've proposed a spiritual solution. So you might well ask why I'm now using reason to put forward this circumscribing ethical framework.

The answer is that, unless we have such a framework, our individual efforts to gain spiritual insight into the Good will all clash. We need to be mature enough to keep ourselves from trying to force our perception of goodness onto others, who may have their own perceptions of it. Fortunately, my framework also implies a maturing process, as we'll see.

The seventeeth-century philosopher Thomas Hobbes thought that we human beings establish governments for mutual protection. Since none of us wants to be, say, murdered or robbed, we empower our governments to enact justice on murderers and thieves.

---

[1] I'm aware of criticisms that much seventeenth- and eighteenth-century thought seems archaic by twenty-first-century standards. I'm not proposing that we go back to begone eras; rather, I'm reenvisioning the Enlightenment through a more twentieth-century lens. I see the Enlightenment not as a relic from the past but as an ongoing movement that is still being improved on. As such, we constantly reinterpret it, hopefully with improved vision.

One consequence of this is the rule of law. We ourselves cannot murder or steal, either, because the same government that protects us from murderers and thieves must punish us for murder and theft. A second consequence is that we cannot take the law into our own hands. We have to let the courts decide.

I know that recently there's been a lot of talk about whether or not our law enforcement treats everybody equally. Like many of you, I am very concerned about the injustice I see. We may have different political perspectives, but I think we can all agree that a true free society is one that is nonprejudicial in how it enacts justice.

I also want to make it clear that I'm not proposing to take everything that Hobbes said as good. A lot has changed since the seventeenth century; in Hobbes's time, just challenging the idea that monarchs have some sort of divine right to rule was a huge step toward self-governance. Today, in our free societies, most of us want democracy, specifically, and not just any type of government.[2] We no longer believe in the medieval concept that God chooses kings by birthright.

Rather, we human beings all have the equal right to participate in self-governance. Our notion of a free society provides us with common virtues that inform how we engage, as a people, within the public forum. But I worry that we're losing sight of those virtues.

The framers of the Declaration of Independence found our unalienable rights in "nature and nature's God." I wonder if part of the problem is that many of us no longer believe in God. Since today's science also teaches us to understand nature as mindless, we have lost the grounding for that statement, both in God and nature. I wonder if we need to transplant our notions of unalienable rights into firmer ground.

Just as we need our government to enforce laws to protect us, our democracies also require each citizen to have certain rights. We all need to have freedom of expression in order to share our political opinions. We need freedom of religion and a separation of church and state to ensure that no theocracy (or its ideological equivalent) comes to power, to dominate all of us and pound out with an iron fist all our individual searches for ethics.

We need equality, so that everyone is equally represented. From equality arises equal justice, equal rights, and the right to be treated with respect and dignity by the government, including by our justice

---

2 I'm using the term *democracy* very broadly here to include democratic republics such as the United States. In other words, all I mean by the term is a government of the people, by the people, and for the people. However, I do recognize that there are ways some of our republics could be more democratic. For example, the United States could pass a constitutional amendment to make the election of the president based directly on popular vote rather than through the Electoral College.

system and by law enforcement. These rights must be unalienable, and the laws our governments make must not oppress them.[3]

It's a classic view of Enlightenment philosophy that each of these rights implies a duty. We have the duty to respect other people's freedom of expression, our great diversity of religion, and everyone's essential equality. From these rights and duties arise the following virtues:

1. **Tolerance:** Respecting the free expression and freedom of religion of others.
2. **Courage:** Speaking up for what we believe in, even if others threaten us with abuse.
3. **Listening:** There are two sides to the free speech coin: speaking and listening. While it's our civic duty to speak our minds, we all need to make space for others to speak theirs.
4. **Understanding:** Because different people have different ethics, values, ideologies, and political philosophies, we need to try to understand their assumptions, reasoning, and perspectives so that we can communicate with them.
5. **Self-Discipline:** We must have the self-discipline to tolerate, understand, listen, be courageous, and do everything we ought to do in the public forum.
6. **Egalitarianism:** Just as everyone must be equal under the law, so should we treat everyone else as essential equals.
7. **Politeness:** Part of respecting the opinions of others is to respond to them in a nonabusive and relatively peaceful way. We'll always have heated arguments, but these can be mitigated by politeness. Politeness is a balance between rudeness and passivity with regard to expressing our opinions.
8. **Honesty:** In order to argue against a political opponent, we must be honest both about our opinions and theirs. It's wrong to twist your opponent's words just to win, because society needs a fair trial of both opinions. It's equally wrong to claim to have opinions you don't actually have just to get people on your side.
9. **Love for Our Fellow Citizen:** I use *citizen* extremely broadly here to include immigrants of all sorts as well as official citizens. Equality implies a certain type of friendliness and kindness to everyone in our society. So we should feel friendly toward them and maybe have a sense of *agape*.
10. **Love for Our Political Opponents:** This is a hard one that takes a great deal of courage and self-discipline. Since our political opponents are fellow citizens, democracy entails extending our

---

[3] Part of how I see us reenvisioning the Enlightenment is to include human rights alongside natural rights. Thus, the right to be treated with respect and dignity goes alongside the right to freedom of religion, for example.

love for our fellow citizens even to them. None of these democratic virtues mean anything if we only extend them to people we agree with.[4]

I reject the idea that "there can be no peace." We can avoid tribalism, not by agreeing on everything, but rather by understanding our duties outside of our own echo chambers. By following these virtues, we arise as beings better than the brutes nature made us. These virtues forge us into citizens. While we still have our disparate, often opposing, ideologies, as citizens we must set selfishness and tribal loyalty aside to act for the good of our society, to allow our fellow citizens to do the same, and to comport ourselves well within the public forum.

All this implies personal growth. From individuals, we arise as citizens, but we're still individuals inside. That's a very important thing that I believe our free societies should foster. We're precious and sacred beings because we are each unique. We are special, not in the sense of being greater than anyone else, but in the sense of each having our own unique sacredness. As citizens, we grow beyond mere individuals, but the individual is still contained within the citizen. Being a citizen means more to me than just a citizen of a nation. It could be a citizen of a state or province, a city, a church, a school, or even of a game table or a circle of friends. In all cases, the same virtues apply.

From here, I'd like to continue from mere citizenship in each of these groups, to apply the same virtues to the whole world. Just as individuals arise as citizens, so citizens arise as *cosmopolitans*. The word *cosmopolitan* literally means *citizen of the world* in Greek (*cosmos* = world, *politan* = citizen). The way I'm using it, becoming a cosmopolitan does not mean abandoning citizenship, any more than becoming a citizen implies losing one's individuality. We can still work for the common good of our country, state, province, municipality, social group, and so on, while remaining mindful of the needs of the whole world.

We can do what we each think is best for the world without jettisoning our citizenship in any type of society or getting rid of our own individuality and unique vision of goodness. So we can simultaneously act as individuals, citizens of multiple groups, and cosmopolitans.

---

4 Of course, I don't mean to condone violent protests or riots. The political opponents we should respect are those operating within the law and according to free-society values. We won't always have to get along with our opponents either, because we're likely to find their views repugnant. I mean that we should still treat them with respect and dignity, so long as they're willing to uphold the same free-society values that we are. This takes a great deal of self-discipline. It's something to strive toward. And we should still oppose them, just in a polite way.

Now, you may well ask why we should care about being citizens or cosmopolitans. Many of us today may well feel estranged from our nation states. We may feel tempted to *just* be individuals. In Chapter 1, I expressed my opinion that ethics is about relationships *among* people, rather than just about individual people. If you were the only person in the universe, you wouldn't need ethics to tell you how you ought to behave, just hedonism to tell you how to be happy.

Ethics, therefore, involves all of us together. I would argue that it's impossible for us to be ethical *only* as individuals. To be *only* an individual is, in essence, to be a sociopath: a person without any regard for their *relationships* with others. To be ethical, on the other hand, implies regard for those relationships. Relationships imply society. Society implies citizenship. When that society is the whole world, it implies cosmopolitanism (as I've defined it).

I believe that what I'm describing, in my idea that we should all grow from individual to citizen to cosmopolitan, is a teleology for a free society. Our virtues are implied by this teleology, because they are the virtues necessary for us to make this growth. It's hard work, and it will take practice—and a lot of getting outside of our comfort zones—but I know we're up to the task.

Glossary

I've provided this handy glossary to look up terms I've used in the book. These are not meant to match the quality or content of encyclopedia entries, but are meant only to help you, the reader, remember various subjects as I use them in the book.

Categorical Imperative
The ethical idea, put forward by Immanuel Kant, that before we begin any action, we should ask if we can will it as a universal law for everyone. In other words, *how would it be if we all did that?* So before you, let's say, punch a guy you don't like in the nose, you should ask yourself how it would be if we all punched people we didn't like. We probably answer that we wouldn't want others to behave that way toward us, so we can conclude that it's unethical to punch people in the nose, even if we don't like them.

Darwin, Charles
Lived 1809–1882. English scientist who did groundbreaking research on the science of evolution and proposed a theory to explain it: the theory of natural selection. I think it changed how we view God (or even whether we believe in God), because before Darwin it was easy to assume that various forms of life, such as birds, must have been designed to be the way they are. Darwin pointed out that they need not have been. They might have simply changed over millions of years of evolution.

Dyad
The second layer of the Tetractys. The second of Pythagoras's four perspectives on reality. This is the perspective in which everything is understood as Platonic Forms, essences, or abstractions. There is Right-triangle-ness, because the Pythagorean theorem proves a common essence of all right triangles. There is Apple-ness, because apples are the fruit of a type of tree that can be categorized by biologists. Thus, two apples from two different trees are both apples, rather than two completely unrelated objects.

Kant, Immanuel
Lived 1724–1804. German Enlightenment philosopher from the eighteenth century. Kant's book *Foundation of the Metaphysic of Morals* introduces his concept of the categorical imperative. In that same book, Kant assumes that nature has a will and a purpose given by God and that nature has, in turn, given us reason so that we can figure out what it means to be ethical.

Monad
The first layer of the Tetractys. The first of Pythagoras's four perspectives on reality. This is the perspective in which everything is one big continuum. We're all part of one whole. There's no point at which I end and the cosmos begins or where the cosmos ends and you begin. Therefore, from this perspective, I cannot really speak of me as separate from you and you cannot really speak of yourself as separate from me.

Plato
Lived 424–348 BCE. The ancient Greek philosopher who came up with the idea of the Platonic Form.

Platonic Form
The philosophical idea, first suggested by the ancient Greek philosopher Plato, that there are essential or ideal things—most of us today would probably say *abstractions*. Common examples include Beauty, Love, and Justice. Plato often stated these in terms like *Love itself by itself* or *Justice itself by itself*. Right-triangle-ness, the essence that all right triangles share, can be thought of as the Platonic Form of right triangles, and that may be one example of a Platonic Form because of the Pythagorean theorem.

I don't know whether I agree with Plato on all of this. For example, I tend to think that beauty is in the eye of the beholder. But I do believe in a Platonic Form of Good. I don't really have a robust, rational argument for it, but I've thought about this extensively enough to convince myself that it's plausible.

Pythagoras
Lived 570–495 BCE. The ancient Greek philosopher credited with discovering both the Pythagorean theorem and the Tetractys.

Pythagorean Theorem
The Pythagorean theorem is the mathematical proof that for any right triangle (that is, a triangle with one angle of ninety degrees), where x and y are the lengths of the two sides forming the ninety-degree angle and z is the length of the hypotenuse, or diagonal side, that $x^2 + y^2 = z^2$.

I use this to explain what a Platonic Form is. I think that formula is evidence for a Platonic Form of Right-triangle-ness, since it expresses a quality that all right triangles share, regardless of how big they are or what angles they have.

Tetractys
The Tetractys is the concept, proposed by the Greek philosopher Pythagoras, that there are four levels at which we can understand reality. Though it has been conceptualized differently at different eras, these changes in understanding of the Tetractys come about mainly because of new understandings about reality. Various mystical ideas have also accrued to it at times that I'm not using in this book.

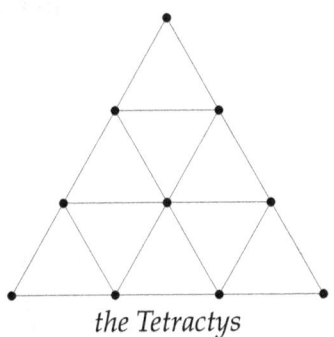

the Tetractys

The four levels of reality are numbered starting with the most abstract and transcendent, the Monad, and going down to the most manifest and material, the Tetrad. These levels are:

Level	Formal Name	Description
1	Monad	All is one and one is all. Unity. The One. The Good.[1]
2	Dyad	Reality as abstractions, essences, Platonic Forms.
3	Triad	Our model of the material world, symbols, numbers, geometry. The blueprints of the material world.
4	Tetrad	The material world in all its messiness.

All four levels of reality are going on simultaneously. They are all true all the time. I use the Tetractys as a central theme in this book, because I think it's a useful piece of wisdom. I think it's important to be careful to think through how we today understand those four levels of reality, since modern science may cause us to think it through a little differently.

---
[1] I put the Platonic Form of Good at the Monad, rather than at the Dyad with the other Forms, because I believe Plato thought of the Good as the Form from which all other Forms are derived.

Still, I think it's a powerful tool for thinking about reality. For example, the ancient Greek philosophers thought that matter was composed of fire, water, earth, and air, and so they made much ado about them on the Tetractys. However, we now know that matter is composed of the elements of the periodic table. We can still use the Tetractys without the four elements, though. I think you can probably have Platonic Forms within Platonic Forms, too. For example, you could have Dog within Mammal, Mammal within Animal, and Animal within Life, and so on.

Also, we don't necessarily know the truth. Our models of reality may be false. I don't think this means the Tetractys is not useful, though. For example, biologists used to say that the species of dog is *canis familiaris*, but they've recently discovered that dogs share so many genes with wolves that they are now considered to be the same species, *canis lupus*. This does not mean that there isn't a Platonic Form of Dog-ness. Biologists are convinced that they've categorized things in a better way that more authentically models nature. It's we who were wrong, not Dog-ness. This is because our perceptions are imperfect, rather than because there isn't a truth out there.

Categorization does not necessarily make something a Platonic Form. It's only a Platonic Form if that category refers to a real essence, such as it is with right triangles. So it's important to be aware of categorization and abstraction that doesn't accurately model reality.

Tetrad

The fourth layer of the Tetractys, or Pythagoras's fourth perspective on reality. Understanding reality in terms of the material world, the way scientists typically do. At this level, for example, there are no right triangles, because right triangles represent spatial coordinates. This way of looking at reality only looks at it in terms of the actual matter that everything is composed of (as well as the space between that matter, of course).

Three apples aren't understood as three, because that would entail representing the apples in terms of a number, which would require us to understand reality in terms of the Triad. The apples in question cannot even really be categorized at this level because each is different. In order to categorize them biologically, we would need to realize that all apples come from trees of a common grouping of species, which would require the Dyad. So at the purely material level, all we can say about three apples is that there are these things that will fit in our hands and that we can eat them. That is, at this level, they are only understood as raw matter.

Triad
The third layer of the Tetractys, or Pythagoras's third perspective on reality. Understanding reality as represented by numbers, geometric shapes, and the like. For example, a right triangle exists spatially, but not materially. It's not made up of matter. When counting, say, three apples, the concept of the number three does not exist in the actual pile of apples, but it does exist *as* the number of apples.

Bibliography

Aristotle, *Nicomachean Ethics*
Bonewits, Isaac, *Neopagan Rites*
Bonewits, Isaac, *Real Magic*
Campbell, Joseph, *The Hero with a Thousand Faces*
Gardner, Gerald, *Witchcraft Today*
Hutton, Ronald, "Paganism in the Missing Centuries" in *Witches, Druids, and King Arthur*
Hutton, Ronald, *Triumph of the Moon*
Iamblichus, *On the Mysteries*
Johnston, Sarah Iles, *Hekate Soteira*
Kant, Immanuel, *Foundations of the Metaphysics of Morals*
MacIntyre, Alasdair, *After Virtue*
MacIntyre, Alasdair, *A Short History of Ethics*
Mill, John Stuart, *Utilitarianism*
Moore, Thomas, *A Religion of One's Own*
Plato, *Gorgias*
Plato, *Timaeus*
Sallustius, *On the Gods and the World*
Shaw, Gregory, *Theurgy of the Soul: The Neoplatonism of Iamblichus*
Vervaeke, John, "Awakening from the Meaning Crisis" video series
Watts, Alan, various lectures

About the Author

Ivan Richmond grew up as a child in the Green Gulch branch of San Francisco Zen Center, where his father served as a Zen priest. He received a BA in Greco-Roman Classics from Reed College in 1996. In 2001, he joined the Wiccan and Pagan community. He was ordained as a priest in the Waxing Moon tradition in 2005 and Gardnerian tradition in 2009, both by Valerie Voigt. He currently has a 3rd degree in both traditions and is the High Priest of Waxing Moon Circle and Temple of Inanna and Dumuzi, both in San Jose, CA. He is the author of two books, including this one. His first book, *Silence and Noise: Growing up Zen in America*, Atria Books, 2003 is about his childhood in San Francisco Zen Center.

About Concrescent Scholars

Concrescent Scholars is dedicated to peer-reviewed works of scholarship in the fields of Esotericism, Pagan religion and culture, Magic, and the Occult from within, and without, the Academy.

These young scholarly fields intersect in real lives today and need a forum in which to mature. This is one such forum where the voices of both academic and the practitioner will be heard in new collections, monographs, and translations that further the discipline.

We take advantage of the recent revolution in publishing technology and economics to bring forth works that, previously, might only have been circulated privately, or been prohibitively expensive.

Now, we are growing the future together.

Colophon

This book is made of Palatino, using Adobe InDesign. The cover was designed by Noah Fischer and the body was set by Sam Webster.

Visit our website at
http://Concrescent.press

www.ingramcontent.com/pod-product-compliance
Lightning Source LLC
Chambersburg PA
CBHW050635160426
43194CB00010B/1684